CULTURALLY RELEVANT STORYTELLING
IN QUALITATIVE RESEARCH

NEW DIRECTIONS FOR THEORIZING IN
QUALITATIVE INQUIRY
A BOOK SERIES EDITED BY NORMAN K. DENZIN
AND JAMES SALVO

New Directions for Theorizing in Qualitative Inquiry consists of thematically edited volumes that help us understand the philosophical concepts undergirding theory and how to put theory into practice to bring about social justice. The chapters in each volume, from established and emerging scholars and largely drawn from papers at the annual International Congress of Qualitative Inquiry, represent new directions for incorporating theory into justice-oriented qualitative research. Taking particular interest in theorists who haven't yet had mainstream influence, the series is designed to reach a wide audience of scholars and students in the humanities and social sciences, including those seasoned in the philosophical language of theory and novices to theoretically-oriented research. The series aims to bring about experimental ways of reading lives to implement radical social change.

Books in the Series:
New Directions In Theorizing Qualitative Research: The Arts (2020)
New Directions In Theorizing Qualitative Research: Indigenous Research (2020)
*New Directions In Theorizing Qualitative Research:
Performance as Resistance* (2021)
New Directions In Theorizing Qualitative Research: Theory as Resistance (2021)
*Qualitative Research in the Time of COVID: Lessons Learned and Opportunities
Presented During a Pandemic* (2023)
*Culturally Relevant Storytelling in Qualitative Research: Diversity, Equity, and
Inclusion Examined through a Research Lens* (2024)
*Educational Media and Technology: New Developments in Remote Teaching,
Machine Learning, Artificial Intelligence and Other Topics* (2024)
*Education and Sustainability: Applying the United Nations' 17 Sustainable
Development Goals to Teaching and Learning* (2024)

If you have a manuscript or a proposal for a book-length work, please send it to Norman Denzin (n-denzin@illinois.edu) or James Salvo (salvo3000@gmail.com). All books published by MEP are peer reviewed. We will acknowledge receipt of your material but it may be 4-6 weeks before we can provide initial feedback about your proposal.

CULTURALLY RELEVANT STORYTELLING IN QUALITATIVE RESEARCH

೧೦ Diversity, Equity, and Inclusion Examined through a Research Lens

EDITED BY NORMAN K. DENZIN
AND JAMES SALVO

Myers Education Press
Gorham, Maine

Myers Education Press

Copyright © 2024 | Myers Education Press, LLC
Published by Myers Education Press, LLC
P.O. Box 424
Gorham, ME 04038

All rights reserved. No part of this book may be reprinted or reproduced in any form or by any electronic, mechanical, or other means, now known or hereafter invented, including photocopying, recording, and information storage and retrieval, without permission in writing from the publisher.

Myers Education Press is an academic publisher specializing in books, e-books and digital content in the field of education. All of our books are subjected to a rigorous peer review process and produced in compliance with the standards of the Council on Library and Information Resources.

Library of Congress Cataloging-in-Publication Data available from Library of Congress.

13-digit ISBN 978-1-9755-0518-9 (paperback)
13-digit ISBN 978-1-9755-0519-6 (library networkable e-edition)
13-digit ISBN 978-1-9755-0520-2 (consumer e-edition)

Printed in the United States of America.

All first editions printed on acid-free paper that meets the American National Standards Institute Z39-48 standard.

Books published by Myers Education Press may be purchased at special quantity discount rates for groups, workshops, training organizations and classroom usage. Please call our customer service department at 1-800-232-0223 for details.

Cover design by Teresa Lagrange.

Visit us on the web at **www.myersedpress.com** to browse our complete list of titles.

Contents

INTRO DEI as Ethics: A Boundless
Conceptualization of Universal Accessibility   1
James Salvo

ONE Storying for Diversity, Equity, Inclusion,
and Justice in Education   9
*Tanja Burkhard, DaVonna Graham, Fatima Brunson,
and Valerie Kinloch*

TWO Ating Kuwento/Nuestro Testimonio:
Storytelling as Knowledge Creation, Collective
Consciousness, and Cultural Empowerment
for Researchers from Diverse Backgrounds   25
Ricardo Montelongo and Pat Lindsay Catalla-Buscaino

THREE "We Know Who We Are": A Métis Digital
Storytelling Project During COVID-19   41
Robert Henry, Chelsea Gabel, and Amanda LaVallee

FOUR With My Ancestors in My Studio:
Researching My Taíno Roots   57
Leslie C. Sotomayor II

FIVE Do No Harm: An Autoethnography of
a Novice Research Supervisor Learning
to Dwell Within and Stand Apart   75
Joanne Yoo

SIX Unmaking Frames through Poetic
Photographic Inquiry: When Silence Meets
Art Meets Method Meets Resistance   89
Reyila Hadeer

SEVEN Here We Go Again: Three Narratives of
Struggle to Disrupt Racial Dominance in
Education Spaces   101
Rae Fox-Charles, Thong Vang, and Asha Omar

EIGHT Culturally Competent Teachers in Action
in an Urban-Multicultural Classroom
through a Qualitative Research Lens   115
Benedict Adams

NINE Being Stuck: Autoethnographically
En-gender-ing an Anti-sexist
Teaching Praxis   133
Aaron Teo

TEN Critical Disability Studies as Methodologies
for Social Change: The Use of Participatory
Research Methodologies in Social Research
with Women and Girls with Disabilities
in the Global South   147
*Xuan Thuy Nguyen, Tammy Bernasky, Marnina Gonick,
and Claudia Mitchell*

About the Authors   *167*

Index   *171*

INTRODUCTION

 # DEI as Ethics: A Boundless Conceptualization of Universal Accessibility

James Salvo

A BORROMEAN KNOT CONSISTS OF THREE closed rings linked together in such a way that no set of two rings are linked, but only stay together as part of a linked structure, owing to the positioning of the remaining ring. Cut any ring of the structure, and the remaining two rings fall away from each other. In other words, the three rings are linked together such that all the rings are equally important to the structure's integrity.

I think this can be a useful way to think about diversity, equity, and inclusion (DEI). Each of these is a ring in a Borromean knot, the knot itself being accessibility. No two of these components of accessibility are conceptually synonymous or redundant, and there's no accessibility unless diversity, equity, and inclusion are connected in such a way that all are equally important to the structure. Cut away any of the components, and the integrity of accessibility is lost.

This, however, is a spatial metaphor. Temporally speaking, though, how might we understand diversity, equity, and inclusion in a way that might persist throughout time? It's true that political contexts can change, but does this mean that what we mean by diversity, equity, and inclusion must change along with these contexts? I think our understandings of diversity, equity, and inclusion ought to continue to develop as we collectively come to know how the three interact to create accessibility. I think we're in the process of coming to this understanding, and we're not yet finished with this epistemological project. However, I do believe that if we continue to think together, it's indeed possible to come to an understanding that can apply in all contexts. In other words, I don't think it's an impossible goal to have a general understanding of how diversity, equity, and inclusion can be knotted together, knotted eternally such that DEI itself isn't always already context dependent.

To work toward a context-independent understanding of diversity, equity, and inclusion, I think we need to be cautious about suturing any of these concepts to the particularities of any specific political project. For instance, I'm old enough to remember a time wherein in an academic context, let's say, there were entire disciplines dominated by white men, whole departments at particular universities sometimes consisting of white men only. As I remember, the philosophy department where I did my undergrad was one such department. At that time, what would've counted as an adequate gesture toward diversity was to maybe consider hiring a woman. We've at least come far enough to realize the woeful inadequacy of this particular attitude. We know to look beyond the one demographic category, and we know that that particular demographic category itself is far from binary. In the current political context, we might add to our consideration more categories that are in keeping with an ever-increasing recognition of political subjectivities. But still, how can we be sure that we're not leaving out any political subjectivity unfairly, not because we're deliberately bigoted in some way, but only because we've collectively been unable to recognize that a certain subjectivity exists?

I think we might come to understand that political frameworks are not particularly well adapted to realizing all the subject positions that exist within their respective polities. I think this might be for the reason that political subjectivities and the requests that go along with them can often go unnoticed without a critical mass of recognitions of these subjectivities, and this is of course to the detriment of those subjectivities while they persist to be unrecognized. Once recognized, and with enough time, we can wonder things such as, "How could people back in the day have missed something so obvious?" But still, if the point is not to miss anything because we want to be as fair as possible, retroactive regret is of little use. So if we'd like to anticipate what we've overlooked without treating critical mass recognition as a necessity, then we're left to rely upon our limited imaginations when seeking to add to our list of recognized subjectivities. True, we're entering an era of machine intelligence that can help us identify unrecognized subjectivities, but the iterations of machine intelligence that are trained on human discourse would reproduce at least some of our lack of imaginative capacity.

At this point, I think we might identify at least two issues. The first is that it could be that we're encountering the problem of a Hegelian bad infinity when we seek to remedy the situation in an additive way. Second, I think it might be a mistake to absolutely frame DEI as a political project to begin with.

What's the problem of a Hegelian bad infinity? For Hegel, thinking about the infinite as a perpetually additive phenomenon is illogical. Just as adding together any innumerable amount of zeros never gets you to anything more than zero, at the end of the day, plus one forever and ever relies upon finite ones, so how could any number of finite ones add up to something infinite? Rather, the logical way to think of the infinite isn't as additive, but as something that's conceptually boundless, something that's the opposite of the bound finite, something that doesn't consist of finitude innumerable, but something that's different from finitude altogether. And if we apply this notion of the infinite as boundless to the infinite possibility of recognizable political subjectivities, this could potentially solve the problem of leaving out any subjectivities we haven't yet added for lack of imagination. The point becomes to have never excluded those subjectivities to begin with, because we start from a position of openness. However, to think about the political in this infinite as boundless way is to think beyond the political itself, for this would exceed the necessarily finite borders of polities with finite populations. To think about the political as boundlessly infinite is to push politics toward an absolute wherein it transforms into something else. That something else is ethics.

And this is why I suggest that DEI—at least as a foundation for universal accessibility—is perhaps not a political project in the way we typically conceive of politics. As typically conceived, the political addresses political requests as they arise. In this way, it's bound by an a posteriori empiricism: You don't know it until it's observed. And though we might try to imagine what might arise, we're nonetheless bound by our limited additive imaginations. We're bound this way because our imaginative starting points within the political are themselves situated within the historical, within what has already come to pass. Thus, I think an appropriate response to critics of DEI who assert that DEI is associated with a political agenda, one not their own, would be this: DEI can't be sutured to any particular political agenda because DEI is always already in excess of the political. DEI attempts to think about universal accessibility for ontological beings not from any particular political standpoint, but from that of a eudaimonist ethics. DEI wants to make the flourishing of ontological beings accessible to all. We cannot ignore observation and history—we must definitely pay close attention to both—but we can't think beyond them if we're bound to observation and history as a be-all and end-all. Observation and history as be-all and end-all are limiting inasmuch as they're two things that exhaust potential through the negating and foreclosing activity of actualization. Observation and history pertain to what is and has been. In contrast, if ethics tries to imagine what can and should be, then through openings, eudaimonism attempts to exhaust impotentiality through its universalist aims.

So how might we operationalize DEI as a eudaimonist ethics aimed at universal accessibility? As I said, we need to think together toward this goal. And while offering definitions of diversity, equity, and inclusion might seem to be punctuating the discourse, perhaps starting from logically open understandings is permissible, if only open at one end. In other words, leaving what they are as open for exploration, there are perhaps some things that we can agree on regarding what diversity, equity, and inclusion are not, at least in terms of how they aren't bound and what they necessarily exclude. I offer some of my own understandings here.

First, I think it's useful to understand diversity as being unbound by any particular set of categories. Without categories, the universe is an otherwise all-inclusive, undifferentiated oneness. Diversity is what we discover in the universe when we use our capacity to negate through language and carve out what we consider to be plural individuals from the universal oneness, *universal* here meaning *belonging to the universe that is but one*. In the vast universe, literally speaking, nothing that can be circumscribed as individual is the same as anything other than itself. Even then, philosophically speaking, the persistence of self-identity isn't without its problems. In any case, because it's true that diversity is what there is to be discovered, it becomes of concern should we find any type of observably categorizable and unfair homogeneity in institutional, social, or political contexts smaller than the universe. If we can describe a population writ large as diverse in a particular way, in a smaller institutional, social, or political sample of that population, given that the sample is large enough, we might expect to find that same describable diversity. When we instead find unexpected types of homogeneity in institutional, social, or political contexts, we might ask whether or not this serves some purpose. If we find that the purpose this homogeneity serves is to uphold oppression through harm, unfair abandonment, privilege, supremacy, or bigotry, then we need to do something about it. We need to do something about such a situation because it isn't equitable.

Second, we might consider equity as being unbound by any particular notion of fairness, considering it to be an infinite openness to what any ontological being might request as a reasonable aim toward fairness in general. We know that equal doesn't necessarily mean fair, so equity must be universal not in the sense of one-size-fits-all—a concept that's rightly criticized—but be universal in a way that's universally open to any necessary process of fairness, to any process of fairness made necessary by the diversity that belongs to the one that is the universe. This, I believe, is the most useful understanding of *universal rights*, rights that are best suited to the all-at-once singular and pluriform being of the universe. As per above, because the universe is discoverably diverse, the fair processes upholding rights must match the diversity of the ontological beings to whom those rights belong. Again, this isn't one-size-fits-all universalism, but a conception of the universal that entails—in whatever ways one circumscribes the concept of oneness—one-to-one correspondence with all the beings of the universe. So here, somewhat counterintuitively, pursuing equity is a context-independent pursuit, this because to remain universal, it's necessarily *always* the case that equity be considered case-by-case. Contexts are typically understood to apply to cases that are more than one. If contexts lose generality altogether and extend to a universal situation, then we're thinking about the absolute context, the context that passes over into the all-encompassing context of the boundlessly conceptualizable particularities that make up what we know as the universe. Thus, a universal conception of equity is inclusive at the level of the individual, in the sense of an individual's being whatever it may be.

Third, we might consider inclusion as that which excludes only the unfairly exclusive. If it's the case that we're owed something as ontological beings, then it must also be the case that as ontological beings who are singular in the plural, we owe something to others. The unfairly exclusive shirks this responsibility and excludes through oppressions perpetrated through harm, unfair abandonment, privilege, supremacy, and bigotry. Inclusion, then, is boundless in the direction of necessarily including the equitable, the only ends closed off being those ends working against equity itself. Furthermore, inclusivity as it pertains to the being of the universe is the concept by which we understand the universe to be both singular and absolutely plural in its makeup. Without inclusivity, diversity isn't a legible concept pertaining to the universe.

If we put these three considerations together, we might better understand how DEI is a Borromean knot. Diversity and inclusion are otherwise boundless, but if universal accessibility is the target, both must be bound by the concept of equity as fairness, for the universe in its diversity includes beliefs, values, and practices that are harmful, unfairly abandoning, privileging, supremacist, and bigoted. Still, boundless equity and inclusion can only be if both are bound by an attendance to the kind of diversity that exists in the universe, a diversity wherein the largest unit of recognition is the conceptualizable individual. Any unit larger than the individual becomes reductive of the individual. Further, though we may find it necessary to speak of oppressed groups when it comes to systematic oppression, we ourselves don't necessarily want to partake in the reductiveness that allows for the systematicity of an oppression that refuses to acknowledge diversity at the level of individuals. Systematic oppression, we should note, promotes an ideological fantasy that the oppressed are but a faceless, undifferentiated same in order to support the mechanism of its oppression. And finally, equity and diversity only work together as boundless if both are bound by an inclusivity such that the only exclusion is the unfairly exclusive. Knotted so, universal accessibility cannot be without this tripartite structure as its foundation.

Is DEI a sufficient condition for universal accessibility? Perhaps we'll find more necessities as we continue to work toward the flourishing of all ontological beings. Nonetheless, I think we'll indeed find time and again that DEI is a necessary condition with respect to any eudaimonist project of ethics.

The chapters in this volume take issues of diversity, equity, and inclusion as necessary conditions for universal accessibility. As the author of the introduction to such a collection, I have the luxury of speaking and philosophizing in universal generalities, in generalities involving the universe as a whole. However, the work of DEI must necessarily be attendant to particularities that are non-coterminous with the universe. For one thing, just as humans touch the earth for most of their lives, DEI as it pertains to humans is grounded to the world. Universal as our understandings may aspire to be, the way to these aspirations is always through the lived experience of those of whom and for whom we write. Without educational tellings and retellings of stories about these lived experiences, when it comes to an ability to flourish, accessibility for all wouldn't be possible. It wouldn't be possible because the flourishing of all entails an epistemological component: In order to ethically make decisions about how we should live, we need to know how we do live. Because we're imaginatively limited ontological beings who aren't epistemically omniscient, we need to listen to one another so that we may engage in the epistemological tessellation necessary to even make attempts at a "for all." To this end, while being respectfully attendant to the political necessities of observation and history, but not being bound to either as foreclosing agents that don't let us imagine ways forward, the present volume fits together shared stories of lives, shared stories that invite us to consider, as a matter of ethical concern, what can and should be.

Chapter Summaries

Considering people to be "storied beings," Tanja Burkhard, DaVonna Graham, Fatima Brunson, and Valerie Kinloch open this volume by exploring storying as a methodological framework. From their research emerge critical stories about teaching for diversity, equity, and justice, including narratives about some of the difficulties reserved for educational and research spaces that intentionally center DEIJ work.

Ricardo Montelongo and Pat Lindsay Catalla present their qualitative methodology centered upon using storytelling in studies involving Filipino and Mexican American communities. They wish to use their scholarship to help those with their shared backgrounds understand how their race and ethnicity have been deployed in creating change, both educational and societal. They pay particular attention to the language of stories.

With respect to many Métis people in Canada, Robert Henry, Chelsea Gabel, and Amanda LaVallee note the effects of intergenerational trauma and continued settler colonialism with respect to the loss of identity, culture, and language. Still, despite the historical and contemporary exclusion from Canadian society, Métis identities, cultures, and understandings of relationality persist through shared stories. Paying particular attention to research ethics, their chapter explores the digital storytelling process through the COVID-19 pandemic with Métis youth, adults, and elders whose familial connections are to the Métis homeland, which includes Manitoba, Saskatchewan, and Alberta.

Leslie Christina Sotomayor discusses Gloria Anzaldua's theories of *conocimiento* and *autohistoria-teoría*, putting forth a theoretical framework for bridging spaces, spaces that embody an in-between space. Sotomayor documents a generative way of theorizing history and self through an art studio process and a feminist writing practice of visual testimonios.

Next, five chapters are epistemologically focused. Joanne Yoo encourages us to explore inclusive ways of knowing. She encourages us to understand how our words and actions might impact others. Reyila Hadeer reminds us how voices can be drowned out and urges us toward reconsiderations of inclusivity by considering the photographic frame as a concept. Rae Charles Harge, Thong Vang, and Asha Omar explore epistemological alternatives and a way toward generative dialogue regarding the reception and implementation of culturally relevant pedagogy. Starting with a useful account of the philosophical foundations of education in the United States, Benedict Adams offers us an extended epistemological reflection on cultural competency. Aaron Teo offers us a sustained epistemological reflection on sexism.

This volume closes with a chapter from Xuan Thuy Nguyen, Tammy Bernasky, Marnina Gonick, and Claudia Mitchell. With respect to girls and women with disabilities in the global South, the authors demonstrate the engagement utility of an arts-based, community-engaged, decolonial, and participatory research project.

ONE

Storying for Diversity, Equity, Inclusion, and Justice in Education

Tanja Burkhard, DaVonna Graham, Fatima Brunson, and Valerie Kinloch

AS CO-AUTHORS OF THIS CHAPTER, we—Tanja, DaVonna, Fatima, and Valerie—represent a collective of four Black women educator-researchers who examine critical meanings and uptakes of diversity, equity, inclusion, and justice (DEIJ) within the context of U.S. higher educational institutions. In this chapter, we focus on storying as a methodological framework by first turning the gaze onto critical stories about teaching for DEIJ and about representation that emerged from a mixed undergraduate-graduate course taught by Tanja at a large public research university located in the U.S. Midwest. After Tanja's story, Fatima, one of our co-authors, *restories* aspects of Tanja's story in order to highlight larger reflections for and implications of teaching for DEIJ. Then Valerie engages in another example of storying as a methodological framework by focusing on the challenges and opportunities that present themselves when working to create a shared, collective college-wide vision for DEIJ within this same large public research university. After Valerie's story, Davonna *restories* particular parts of it as a way to emphasize the importance of Black women in leadership roles and institutions listening to and supporting their work. In taking this layered approach to storying as methodology, we explore how participants' stories about DEIJ—from a required university-level course to an assumed college-wide commitment and vision—point to the need to have more critical, engaging contexts, intentions, and commitments to DEIJ work within and across higher education.

In the Fall semester of 2014, Tanja was a second-year graduate student when Valerie became the Chief Diversity Officer and the Associate Dean for the Office of Diversity, Inclusion, and Community Engagement (DICE) in the College of Education at the institution where we both worked and learned. Valerie transformed the dark corner office into a bright and colorful space where many of the graduate students, staff, and faculty of color came to connect. As her advisee, she invited Tanja to join other graduate students and staff to support the office's efforts to promote and engage in equity, diversity, and inclusion across the entire College. Our work was collective and focused on transforming spaces and revolutionizing how we understood, participated in, and interrogated inequities and inequalities that are pervasive within universities and, thus, within the world.

That same semester began with protests across the nation: police officer Darren Wilson fatally shot 18-year-old Michael Brown in Ferguson, Missouri; a few months before Brown was killed, 12-year-old Tamir Rice was killed by police officer Timothy Loehmann only a couple of hours' drive away from our campus. Both murders inspired calls for justice for Black lives in all arenas, including education, but also counter-protests indicative of the polarization that only intensified over the years to come. Under Valerie's leadership, the Office of Diversity, Inclusion, and Community Engagement opened the academic semester with a town hall gathering on Ferguson, which brought together students, faculty, and staff to discuss the uprisings and their implications for the work of our College. Additionally, we decided to implement a research study on Diversity, Equity, and Inclusion (DEI) by recruiting members of our College to provide one-on-one interview data and participate in focus groups that explored our collective and individual DEI experiences. Valerie's work on storying (Kinloch & San Pedro, 2014) as a methodology that is aligned with the goals of humanizing research methodologies provided a framework through which to deeply think about the data we collected, as well as its implications for us as a learning community.

On the one hand, we sought to examine how the pursuit of diversity and inclusion impacts teaching, learning, policy, and cultural understandings for stakeholders in education, their surrounding communities, and throughout education networks, systems, and communities. On the other hand, we sought to investigate how students, faculty, staff, and community members understand and negotiate issues of equity, diversity, and inclusion in their academic, personal, professional, and communal lives. The stories that emerged from this work highlighted vast differences in how students, staff, and faculty experienced their working conditions and leadership. One theme that emerged from a subset of the data was the role played by one department's diversity requirement course. In many ways, the pedagogical, curricular, and positional struggles that came to light related to this course were emblematic of the complexity of DEI work at the College more broadly. Tanja taught sections of this course during her summers as a graduate student at this university. Many of the stories that emerged from the interviews and focus groups she conducted with colleagues highlighted the complicated positioning of the Diversity Requirement Course within the College's DEI landscape. Relatedly, Valerie's facilitation of a position statement that articulated an important historical relevance of DEIJ and that pointed to a vision for taking this work up within our College emphasizes the additional struggles with transforming a place, space, and people to lead for justice.

Theorizing Diversity for Institutional Change

Multicultural education scholars have long advocated for institutional change at both the pK–12 and the university levels. Banks (1993) describes the oftentimes contentious debate surrounding multicultural education of the late 1980s and early 1990s and notes that despite disagreements within the movement for multicultural education, the field has long been concerned with the integration of histories, ways of knowing, and experiences of communities of color and other marginalized communities. He posits: "for multicultural education to be implemented successfully, institutional changes must be made, including changes in the curriculum; the teaching materials; teaching and learning styles; the attitudes, perceptions, and behaviors of teachers and administrators; and the goals, norms, and culture of the school" (Banks, 1993, p. 4). Since many institutions of higher education are still reckoning with aligning their missions, visions, and strategic goals to reflect diversity goals, strategic diversity goal setting, implementation, and documentation thus remains an area of needed growth (Stanley et al., 2019). In her study of how institutions talk about and implement diversity in higher education, Ahmed (2012) notes that diversity is often taken up in ways that maintain the status quo, rather than in ways that work toward a thorough transformation of the ways institutional power operates. For example, she found that many institutions use the language of diversity in ways that do not produce action and change (recruitment or retention of faculty, staff, and students of color; active financial support of students from marginalized communities, etc.). Furthermore, they pursue the development of diversity-based language and initiatives as long as they align with open-to-interpretation terms, such as "excellence." She also notes that many institutions weaponize the language of diversity to thwart accusations of racism and marginalization (see also Hoffman & Mitchell, 2016).

Similarly, many institutions have sought to respond to racist, xenophobic, ableist, and/or anti-LGBTQIA+ incidents on campus or within the larger community by including diversity requirement courses in their curricula (West & Sandoval, 2020). Because of the particular histories of race and (im)migration in the United States, Diversity Requirement Courses (DRC) often become contact zones (Pratt, 1991; Burkhard, 2022) where backlash to the inclusion of historically marginalized perspectives and histories play out. According to Perry et al. (2009), "[t]he diversity-education classroom, in particular, is a site wherein this conflict takes on particular meaning for instructors of color at all academic ranks including graduate teaching assistants and full professors" (p. 81). In PWIs, faculty and graduate students with marginalized identities who are oftentimes champions of diversity and equity, or who are charged with this work, often face the implications of not only being the conveyors and facilitators of knowledge related to *all* marginalized communities, but also become representatives of their own communities.

Speaking for teacher education specifically, Vavrus (2022) notes that "having multicultural concepts incorporated into a teacher education curriculum has been a struggle against an instrumental cookbook approach that unwittingly can align with the far right's relentless attacks on ethnic studies and other multicultural topics" (p. 157). Thus, Diversity Requirement Courses in teacher education are often not only contentious spaces because of the complex histories and ideologies on which they are based, but also because of their positioning within curricula and programs. This is certainly the case for the DRC at the center of storying #1 below (Troubling "Diversity" in Presumably White Settings), and also the case for the movement toward a collective vision/position statement that we describe in storying #2 (Articulating a Position and Forging a Shared Mission).

Context, Site, and Data Sources

The diversity requirement course that Tanja taught emerged as a theme among a subset of participants in our research study. The initial datasets were collected between 2015 and 2017 at a College of Education (*the College*) of a large, Midwestern land-grant institution. According to the College's course catalog, the diversity requirement course in question "focuses on issues of diversity, equity, teacher beliefs, and multicultural education. Emphasis is placed on the roles of identity and lived experience and its influences on approaches to teaching and learning in educational settings." The course is required for all undergraduate and graduate preservice teacher education students and typically taught by one primary instructor and several Graduate Teaching Associates (GTAs). Students enrolled in the course are typically preservice teachers at the upper undergraduate and graduate levels.

As the Chief Diversity Officer (CDO), Associate Dean (AD) of Diversity, Inclusion and Community Engagement (DICE), and Director of the homonymous office, Valerie conceptualized the project to gain deeper insight into understandings and perceptions of DEIJ work in the College and its individual departments. Data consisted of more than 120 in-depth, semi-structured, one-on-one interviews and five focus groups. Many of the participants highlighted the diversity requirement course (DRC) as holding a dual role within the preservice teacher education program, as it functions as an important avenue for discussing social justice themes, but it can also become *the only* place in which these discussions occur. Participants also mentioned the need to have a strong institutional focus on DEIJ, which, in part, led to the co-creation of a position statement.

Storying as Methodology

In developing an analytical approach to the data, we—Valerie, Tanja, Fatima, and DaVonna—spent many hours telling stories about our experiences as Black women in higher education, listening deeply to explore the many ways in which our various experiences connected, and reflecting on moments in time in which we experienced particular ideas differently. In many ways, storying as a methodological framework opened up opportunities to bring our whole selves to the data analysis process. For our purposes, we define storying as the process "that occurs in the space between the telling and listening, the giving and receiving of stories . . ." (San Pedro & Kinloch, 2017, p. 377). Storying as we use it emerges from the larger contexts of Projects in Humanization (PiH), which refers to projects that highlight the importance of stories and storytelling in the pursuit of social justice by centering difference and collaboration. Storying as a methodology can function as a humanizing lens to reflect alongside participants as they react to important events in their lives and how those have changed the ways in which they see themselves and the world around them.

In this way, we consider people to be "storied beings" (O'Toole, 2018, p.175), as their individual stories as well as the ways they are positioned by the stories of institutions are important for understanding social processes. Thus, storying allows us to surface the tensions, conflicts, and emotions related to teaching and leading for DEIJ. By drawing on our own experiences, identities, and ways of knowing, we approached the project and data from an equity lens. However, employing storying as a methodological frame can also be challenging, particularly as we consider the "interweaving and merging process (e.g., braiding, yarning) that occurs in the space between the telling and listening" (San Pedro & Kinloch, 2017) to drive our process of writing and to deepen our approach to listening.

For Black women in particular, storytelling plays a crucial role, as oral histories have sustained us and functioned as a means of validating our knowledge in spaces in which they have been devalued (Collins, 1990). The following stories combine firsthand experiences and reflections from us (Tanja and Valerie) alongside stories from participants, as we worked closely with them throughout the study. Also, they include *restories*, or reflections, from Fatima and DaVonna, both of whom have been immersed in analyzing and re-analyzing research data with Tanja and Valerie. For the DRC course, Tanja was the instructor alongside and under the tutelage of some of the research participants. One participant who, at the time of this study, was an early career faculty member of color in the College and who spoke in great detail about the course, was Nathaniel. As a faculty member of color, his research and teaching centered on critical approaches to equity, diversity, and inclusion. Another focal participant in this same context, Samantha, who identifies as a White woman, was a section teaching assistant and doctoral student. She taught multiple sections of the course both alongside Nathaniel and as the instructor of record. In the next two stories, we present a storied version of the data—from the DRC course and from the crafting of the position statement—by interweaving (San Pedro & Kinloch, 2017) reflections, memories, and quotes from the interview transcripts.

Story 1: Troubling "Diversity" in Presumably White Settings (Storied by Tanja)

On June 17, 2015, Dylan Storm Roof sat in a pew at Emanuel African Methodist Church in South Carolina for several minutes before opening fire and killing nine Black churchgoers. The next day, I (Tanja) entered the first section of the Diversity Requirement Course I was teaching that summer. In this class, we had been talking about race, ethnicity, and education for a few weeks. I remember emotions washing over me as I reviewed the images of Roof's arrest on my phone prior to walking into class, and I invited students to share their thoughts and feelings. One student who, after the first week of class, loudly declared that he simply did not care about the course content and was not planning to teach in a school with racial or ethnic diversity, corrected me when I referred to Roof as "the shooter" rather than "the alleged shooter." He said, "Get it right, Tanja. He has not been prosecuted in a court of law, so you should remember that he is the "alleged shooter." Although I have taught dozens of classes and hundreds of students since, I still remember many of my interactions with this particular student, the grief I felt for the victims at Emanuel African Methodist Church, and the knowledge that there was a particular set of students who were intent on finding flaws with anything I presented in class, the materials we used, and the very foundations of knowledge on which our course was built. "I am a white, middle-class, heterosexual male, and I have never oppressed anyone," he wrote in response to the first reflection assignment that invited students to reflect on their identities, ways of knowing, and upbringing. Teaching this particular class shaped my early understanding of the emotional labor involved in teaching for diversity, equity, and justice, particularly for instructors of color.

When we revisited the data from our project on Diversity, Equity, and Inclusion, I was struck by how much I remember working as a teaching assistant for our Diversity Requirement course being advised by Nathaniel, who was an early career faculty member at the time. Nathaniel was very serious about the course and the direction in which it should be taught. Indeed, in one interview, he mentions the responsibility educators in the program have to engage students in conversations "about identity, about whiteness, about power, about privilege, and engage in discussions about race, racism, equity, inclusion, diversity—the many things that I believe the department is trying to focus on. But I think that we can be a little bit more explicit with that" (Nathaniel, interview). When I reflected on teaching the course and the conversations we had as an Office of Diversity, Inclusion, and Community Engagement, I wondered about Nathaniel's idea that "we can be a little bit more explicit" in our focus on DEI and what exactly this might mean for us as a collective that has expressed an outward commitment to working toward equity. I found that Nathaniel's point, both regarding our responsibility as educators and the need to be more explicit about our focus as a department, speaks to many of the tensions related to DEIJ work. On the one hand, we needed to make curricular choices that address privilege, Whiteness, and race for students in our classes; on the other, many of the activities we included assumed that the audience of our curriculum were White students, oftentimes alienating the few students of color. Reflecting on his definitions of diversity, equity, and inclusion and the student population, Nathaniel describes the following:

> For me, diversity is about. . . . I think diversity and inclusion go hand-in-hand, because oftentimes in institutions it doesn't reflect the population at large. So, for example, when I look in a [DRC course number] classroom and I'm lecturing and I look up—and we always do that survey at the beginning of class asking students of their ethnic identity—and what it breaks down to being is something around 85 to 90 percent of students identify as white, and about 80 percent are female. When I look at pre-service teachers wanting to become teachers, and then I look at [Midwestern City] and the rich diversity that is here, it doesn't match. So, I think that diversity is about including the voices of peoples in our society, of our communities, of our schools into programs and into settings that are historically exclusive of their voices, of their presence, of their identities. [. . .] That's not to say . . . How should I put this? Students tell me that the type of classrooms that they'll end up teaching will likely be 100 percent white. I come back at them and say, even in what appears to be a homogenous population, there is much diversity within that. (Nathaniel, interview session)

Nathaniel not only points out several issues that we had discussed as a department, such as the racial and ethnic mismatch between the overall population of our city and the population of our preservice teachers. He also repeats an idea the student in my class had expressed—namely, the expectation of the preservice teacher education students entering all-White settings after graduating. Nathaniel then troubles this idea by noting the diversity within an assumed homogenous population. Samantha, a doctoral student in the same program and an instructor of the class, echoes his idea, and describes the DRC students' assumptions as follows:

> I think a lot of them come from this idea that they're just going to go back and teach in their same home communities or that they're going to try and teach in

the suburbs. The reality is that, first of all, there might not be jobs for them open there. So if they do end up being in an urban environment, or a more diverse school, and they're not in the mindset or prepared to work with a diverse set of student needs, they're not going to be serving our students well. (Samantha, interview)

Samantha echoes Nathaniel's sense of the collective responsibility of university instructors who teach for equity, as she refers to the future preservice teachers, who were students in our program, will teach as "our students" to be served and troubles students' assumptions that they would teach in exclusively White settings. In my analysis of the data, I was stunned to find that both Nathaniel and Samantha had heard the same sentiment regarding some students' assumptions about the populations they would be working with once in their profession, as well as the way they engaged the course ideas and materials due to this assumption. The presumption of a White audience both by our program and those whom it serves, and by our students and whom they intended to serve, raises a number of questions about the stories we tell (about) ourselves.

Restorying, or Reflecting, on Storying 1: Troubling "Diversity" (Fatima)

As a person focused on discovering the types of professional learning that support actualizing culturally relevant teaching practices, this story reminds me (Fatima) that it remains necessary to engage in relevant and responsive learning activities before relevant and responsive practices can be truly implemented. In my experience as a Black woman who attended a PWI beginning in 2006, I learned that diversity courses can be contentious spaces for various reasons. Without reading and studying the literature, many White students who come from predominantly White neighborhoods may have no reason to think they will be working in schools where the majority of students are racially minoritized.

While I agree that some faculty members' sense of collective responsibility for teaching equity is an antecedent to successfully implementing a DRC, there must be other initiatives in Colleges and Schools within university contexts to support student uptake of and engagement with social justice ideologies. I resonate with Tanja's experience of coming into work moments after an act of racial violence against Black people and then being explicitly challenged by a student who remains resistant to ideas of racial equity and justice. One way to support the inherent emotional labor of DRC instructors and, specifically, of People of Color within these settings, is to provide college-level support structures that address, question, and interrogate social inequities. It is possible that Tanja is the only person in this student's life to address diversity, inclusion, and forms of social inequities and inequalities. And because this is plausible, the University and the College should be charged with addressing these issues. A syllabus that focuses on addressing diversity topics is supported when other syllabi and instructors make it their mission to address diversity-related topics. The story shared by Tanja on "Troubling 'Diversity' in Presumably White Settings" makes me wonder: (1) What types of support structures are present at the University and in the College for DRC instructors? and (2) What other initiatives exist at the University and/or College to support the ideologies being presented in DRC courses and to support students' and instructors' deeper learning and uptake of DEIJ in theory and practice?

Story 2: Articulating a Position and Forging a Shared Mission (Storied by Valerie)

We heeded the call by Nathaniel (see Story 1) to "be more explicit" about our commitments to DEIJ work. In doing so, it became necessary to question the place, the climate, the culture, and the structures that supported and/or ignored critical engagements and institutional practices, procedures, and policies in relation to DEIJ within this same College setting. Thus, under my (Valerie's) leadership, I invited countless students, faculty, and staff members to join me in thinking deeply about what a shared mission and position statement could look like and what it might both include and mean as we reflect on aspects of our past and present, with an eye toward the future of DEIJ work. With approximately 25 people (students, faculty, and staff) agreeing to join this effort, we talked about meanings of diversity, critical; uptakes of equity, the role of inclusion, and the presence of justice in our individual and collective work within the College and in our own personal lives beyond the place where we worked. These talks led to serious discussion, debates, and dialogues that invited us all to dig deep beneath our masks and then deeper underneath our stories of struggle, pain, strife and, in many cases, privilege and racism.

And we dug deep: We shared stories about injustices that we have encountered and/or that someone close to us encountered; we paused in collective silence to catch our breaths, to internally cry, to reflect on how we may have been complicit in injustices and inequalities, and to vow our way into lives of justice and equity.

Every time we came together, we were seated around a large, rectangular table in what was a corner office turned into a bright and welcoming meeting space. We asked ourselves and each other how we saw ourselves, our work, our purpose, and our lives as fundamentally and inextricably connected to, tied to, and bound by unwavering (or, for some, fleeting) commitments to DEIJ. Over time, we openly shared our thoughts in a trusting and critical learning space, and we were able to be forthright about our values, beliefs, and pain. I remember regularly asking the group: "So, what is diversity, equity, inclusion, and justice?" before then saying, "I know these are not easy conversations, and many of us have admitted to not having open opportunities to study and think about these concepts at work." To the latter sentiment, some would reply, "not only at work, but anywhere." So that is where we began—"anywhere" we needed to begin, and this starting place allowed each of us to articulate our ideas however they came out, to refine them in the moment or at another time, to both throw thoughts into the conversation as our streams of consciousness allowed, and to take back those same thoughts in the process of reflecting, revising, and *restorying* our understandings. As our conversations, stories, and processes continued day after day, we moved toward determining how we could best articulate a position and forge a shared vision from our work.

As a literacy and equity scholar, as someone who values the telling and retelling of stories, I always worked to listen intently and intentionally, to allow the pauses and breaks to be a part of the conversations, to look into one's eyes and to feel the energy from one's body as we entered into discussions and debates about what a shared position and vision could look like and might mean not only for our small collective but for the entire College. From what I heard, felt, and saw, I wrote the following (and invited others to revise and add to it), which became part of our position statement titled "Diversity, Equity, and Inclusion: A Position Statement for Colleges of Education":

> We have no other choice but to reject racial injustice, discrimination, prejudice, and hatred. For we know that there are many among us who hate Blackness,

who hate how others self-identify, who hate what others believe, and who hate who others love. They hate collective movements toward freedom, justice, and decolonization, and against racism, sexism, and systemic oppression. Yet we stand lovingly and bravely tall against their hatred. (Kinloch & Collective, 2015)

Opening with a focus on the "urgent need for institutions of higher education in the United States to take a proactive stance with respect to diversity, equity, and inclusion," the position statement was written in a way to encourage us all to examine how "many institutions (schools, universities, the media, the police force, the healthcare industry) have a devastating history with respect to racial oppression, religious persecution, discrimination, and systemic violence." In this examination, we must determine ways to ensure sustainable, engaging, and critical commitments to DEIJ work.

When the final version was completed, it was shared via social media with other Colleges and Schools of Education, with professional organizations, with various higher education leadership groups and equity collaboratives across the nation, and with our own College's leadership team. Many took up the call to not only think deeply about DEIJ within institutional contexts, but to determine tangible ways to reimagine institutions—policies, practices, procedures, and support for people within—into more effective, humanizing, equitable spaces of learning. As facilitators of these efforts, including the writing of a position statement that articulated specific commitments to DEIJ in alignment with our refusal to remain silent and to side with the oppressors, we centered the stories of ourselves (participants and researchers) as well as the stories of our histories and our present moments as we looked to the future of DEIJ work within and beyond institutions of higher education. This work is ongoing and is more necessary now than ever before.

Restorying, or Reflecting, on Storying 2: Articulating a Position (By DaVonna)

Valerie's storying of the creation of a shared position statement is reminiscent of the rich history of collective organizing led by Black women in predominantly White spaces, and in particular, in White educational spaces. Black women, including Valerie as a facilitator of the work described above, are compelled to "be explicit" about our intentions, our visions, our values, and our positionalities in relation to not only our *work* in such a space but our very *being* in White spaces. The tragic irony, as I (DaVonna) see it, is that Black women have historically and contemporaneously been compelled to be explicit as they "reject racial injustice, discrimination, prejudice, and hatred" because our very lives often depended on our outright rejection and resistance. Valerie ushered Black women (and others who participated) through the process of crafting their vision under her leadership as a Black woman within a PWI, who indeed assumed the risks associated with speaking against an otherwise silent institution on issues of DEIJ. The risks are not new to Black women, as speaking up and remaining silent could have similar detrimental outcomes.

Because Black people are often the vanguards leading the push and maintaining the momentum for affecting systems change, PWIs should amplify their voices, research, and leadership while also removing the systemic barriers that make speaking up so risky. The emotional and mental labor of addressing inequities are often thrust upon Black students, faculty, and staff. In contrast, Valerie, a Black woman, felt compelled to lead such change because she (along with other contributors) was willing to use her voice and experiences to ensure that other voices and experiences were heard and taken seriously by institutional leaders. PWIs should work to recruit and retain more Black women from various backgrounds and with multiple identities, providing opportunities for them to share their stories in authentic and humanizing ways that can lead to system-level transformation. Those in positions of leadership and all levels of power are urged to unpack and "sit with" our stories and to work with as well as listen to Black women as we continue to dismantle systems and call out individuals who have maintained the status quo of inequity and inequality.

As Valerie reflected, or storied, her experience as an administrator, professor, and scholar committed to diversity, equity, justice and inclusion, she used stories to reference the past with a vision toward the future (Rooney, Lawlor, and Rohan, 2016). The story she shared on "Articulating a Position and Forging a Shared Mission" allows me to wonder: (1) What supports are needed for more Black women to engage in the critical work of DEIJ within colleges and schools? and (2) What are the obstacles faced by Valerie and other Black women who are leading for transformation with diverse groups of people who might or might not be committed to DEIJ?

Discussion and Conclusion

To build on the hard work of our foremothers and forefathers toward more diverse, equitable, inclusive, and just spaces, we must critically and reflexively listen to each other. This chapter has presented snippets of our work toward this end, as the stories and reflections we have shared are by-products of years of conversations and ruminations on data and in-the-moment experiences that became data. Storying as a framework allowed us to move our lens across space and time, from large macro-contexts to small interactions in a classroom, from the first-person view to the third-person reflection.

We came away from this work with more questions than answers. However, engaging in storying as a group allowed us to contextualize our qualitative data both within the socio-cultural context of anti-Black, state-sanctioned violence and the contexts of our efforts as educators and researchers in the field of education. Like Samantha and Nathaniel, we feel the collective responsibility to work for and on behalf of our students, colleagues, and the young people in their lives and ours. In *Black Feminist Thought: Knowledge, Consciousness, and the Politics of Empowerment,* Patricia Hill Collins (2000) notes that "for Black women new knowledge claims are rarely worked out in isolation from other individuals and are usually developed through dialogues with other members of a community" (p. 260). For many Black women, storying— giving, critically listening to, and reflecting on stories—as a means of knowledge production is one core aspect of knowledge production and validation. As Haddix (2015) argues, in a Black feminist framework, Black women are not only considered knowledge producers but also often share understandings about each other's experiences with racism and sexism that do not have to be made explicit to each other. In other words, "when we complete each other's thoughts and utterances, you nameen. When I do not have to explain myself and use an elaborated code, you nameen" (p. 114). As we continue this work, we acknowledge the important roles of raising our voices and sitting with silences.

References

Ahmed, S. (2012). *On being included: Racism and diversity in institutional life.* Duke University Press.

Banks, J. A. (1993). Multicultural education: Historical development, dimensions, and practice. *Review of Research in Education, 19,* 3–49. https://doi.org/10.2307/1167339

Burkhard, T. (2022). Facing post-truth conspiracies in the classroom: A Black feminist autoethnography of teaching for liberation after the summer of racial reckoning. *Departures in Critical Qualitative Research, 11*(3), 24–39.

Collins, P. H. (2002). *Black feminist thought: Knowledge, consciousness, and the politics of empowerment*. Routledge.

Haddix, M. M. (2015). *Cultivating racial and linguistic diversity in literacy teacher education: Teachers like me*. Routledge.

Hoffman, G. D., & Mitchell, T. D. (2016). Making diversity "everyone's business": A discourse analysis of institutional responses to student activism for equity and inclusion. *Journal of Diversity in Higher Education, 9*(3), 277–289. http://dx.doi.org/10.1037/dhe0000037

Kinloch, V., & San Pedro, T. (2014). The space between listening and storying: Foundations for projects in humanization. *Humanizing Research: Decolonizing Qualitative Inquiry with Youth and Communities, 21*, 42.

O'Toole, J. (2018). Institutional storytelling and personal narratives: Reflecting on the "value" of narrative inquiry. *Irish Educational Studies, 37*(2), 175–189.

Perry, G., Moore, H., Edwards, C., Acosta, K., & Frey, C. (2009). Maintaining credibility and authority as an instructor of color in diversity-education classrooms: A qualitative inquiry. *Journal of Higher Education, 80*(1), 80–105.

Pratt, M. L. (1991). Arts of the contact zone. *Profession*, 33–40.

Rooney, T., Lawlor, K., & Rohan, E. (2016, May). Telling tales: Storytelling as a methodological approach in research. In *ECRM2016-Proceedings of the 15th European Conference on Research Methodology for Business Management: ECRM2016* (p. 225). Academic Conferences and Publishing Limited.

San Pedro, T., & Kinloch, V. (2017). Toward projects in humanization: Research on co-creating and sustaining dialogic relationships. *American Educational Research Journal, 54*(1), Supplement, 373S–394S.

Stanley, C. A., Watson, K. L., Reyes, J. M., & Varela, K. S. (2019). Organizational change and the chief diversity officer: A case study of institutionalizing a diversity plan. *Journal of Diversity in Higher Education, 12*(3), 255–265. https://doi.org/10.1037/dhe0000099

Vavrus, M. J. (2002). *Transforming the Multicultural Education of Teachers: Theory, Research, and Practice* (Vol. 12). Teachers College Press.

West, C. L., & Sandoval, C. L. (2020). Humanizing learning outcomes for diversity requirement courses: Advocating for and supporting social justice education. In *Developing and Supporting Multiculturalism and Leadership Development: International Perspectives on Humanizing Higher Education* (Vol. 30, pp. 15–31). Emerald Publishing Limited.

TWO

Ating Kuwento/Nuestro Testimonio: Storytelling as Knowledge Creation, Collective Consciousness, and Cultural Empowerment for Researchers from Diverse Backgrounds

Ricardo Montelongo and Pat Lindsay Catalla-Buscaino

OUR CHAPTER FOCUSES ON OUR qualitative methodology centered on using storytelling in studies involving Filipino and Mexican American communities. We include individual reflections and mutual thought regarding lessons we learned as a faculty member and doctoral student, respectively, using storytelling in research conducted simultaneously. We aspire to use our scholarship to help those with our shared backgrounds to understand how their race and ethnicity have been discussed and utilized in creating educational and societal change. As of this writing, we are aware of our place within the roles we hold in higher education. As of 2020, approximately 35% of doctorates and 25% of full-time faculty were non-White (National Center for Education Statistics, 2022). As a recent Filipino doctorate recipient and recently tenured Latino faculty member respectively, we converse on how qualitative research has impacted our scholarly and racial and ethnic identities.

Our conversations on the use of storytelling to address diversity, equity, and inclusion topics touched on several important points that we felt are important to share for qualitative researchers. As we further enhanced our research agendas and used our work in advocating for our communities, we asked each other why we pursued qualitative methods for our studies in the first place. This simple, yet critical, question allowed us to deeply self-reflect as researchers of color to understand how our selected methods could influence how our communities are presented and understood. Our self-reflections were shared in dialogues as we pursued work on our research agendas and community leaders. We also paused to ask each other what we were learning about ourselves as qualitative researchers collecting stories from our own communities. We both learned that as researchers, we could not fully detach ourselves from the stories being told to us by our community members. Our own experiences and family histories were being reflected in the data we were collecting for our studies. As researchers from diverse backgrounds, this created a degree of tension between our scholar and ethnic identities. Using stories as primary data, we were often challenged to follow formal researcher positionalities and protocols. Our cultural values of prioritizing empathetic and caring relationships with those we interviewed internalized a sense of inferiority that, as researchers, our scholarship would be judged as invalid or unreliable due to our interest in seeing our research participants as more than data collection points.

While qualitative research provided these challenges, we found that using storytelling in our studies gave us opportunities to critique dominant perspectives on how research is performed and presented. For example, when stories or phrases were presented to us in Spanish or Tagalog, we intentionally kept the stories in the original spoken language to capture their true essence in our studies. For both of us, language was critical to how we presented our participant stories, and we chose to keep those parts of their stories in their original spoken language when present in the narratives. We understood that this went against common practices of translating text to English, but we felt that the receiving of the story in its original language was an important step before studying the content of the story. While receiving our stories in unfamiliar language first adds extra effort for readers, we believe this is how our participants want their stories to be shared and known. In using storytelling, we have learned that their lessons need to be presented in the way they were received by us. As researchers, we understood that long-term memories, especially from our elders, are extremely important. Storytelling provides an outlet to tap into our elders' memories to provide perspectives and descriptions of past injustices and lessons to overcome these barriers.

We reflected on these memories especially from our community elders and recognized from our collected stories that this further complicated the "American" part of our Mexican and Filipino identities. We experienced this complication as we wrote the story of our participants. We questioned whether we are truly documenting our history and collective knowledge appropriately and effectively.

Oral histories told through storytelling are prominent in both our cultures, and we conversed about our challenges of speaking the story compared to writing the story. Oral storytelling captures the emotional context of what is being told, and our challenge as researchers from diverse backgrounds is how to capture that context through written words and descriptions. As we conversed on our research process, we found that the stories in our individual studies empowered not only our participants, but ourselves as well. To further understand these discoveries, we briefly share our own testimonio and kuwento as researchers from diverse backgrounds.

Ricardo's testimonio

I am Dr. Ricardo Montelongo. I tell my students to address me as "Dr. Ric." In the graduate programs where I teach, I intentionally include my title in my nickname to remind students of my educational journey. I come to this space as a third-generation Mexican American who was born and raised in a working-class Texas neighborhood. I am a first-generation college student—undergraduate, master's, and doctorate. I was the first in my family to achieve a doctorate title and the first in our known Montelongo family history to receive this title as of this writing, though hopefully this will change very soon! I continue to evolve in my identities. As of April 2020, I earned tenure with promotion to Associate Professor at my institution.

Since earning tenure, I have developed a research agenda focused on diversity issues in higher education administration, with emphasis on Latina/o/x issues in higher education student affairs. Throughout my over 30 years in higher education, I have seen a noticeable increase in the Latina/o/x representation in the field, with more colleagues aspiring to doctorates and faculty roles. As Latina/o/x representation and engagement within higher education continues to grow, our knowledge should reach well beyond our academic circles. As part of my scholarly identity, I sought out opportunities to highlight how race and ethnicity, especially my own, influence student success, administrative leadership, and campus environments. I am also aware that the educational history of Mexican Americans is not fully represented in the educational curriculums at all levels. Family stories passed down to younger generations have been the primary means of knowledge sharing of past injustices and discrimination of older generations of Mexican Americans in our educational systems.

While my primary focus of study is higher education administration, I always had a yearning to research more intensively this history of educational inequities faced by my ancestors.

Pat Lindsay's kuwento

My name is Dr. Pat Lindsay Carijutan Catalla-Buscaino, and I am known as Pinky in the Asian American Pacific Islander community. I am a first-generation Filipina American daughter of naturalized citizens from the Philippines. Growing up in Southern California, I lived on a street surrounded by my large immigrant Filipino family. Despite financial hardships growing up, there was always an abundance of delicious food, endless stories, and family support. This was my first concept of *bayanihan*, or community spirit, where my origin kuwentos are rooted.

Coming from a lower middle-class household did not stop my parents from giving me and my sister a private Catholic education. They worked extremely hard because they said that our education was the only *pamana*, or inheritance, they could give us as an advantage in the world. I have been a first-generation college student throughout my education—undergraduate, master's, and doctorate. Being the first to go to college in America was daunting because my parents relegated all trust in the private educational institution to tell me how to navigate college. Filipino American families have high expectations of their children to pursue the medical field, especially nursing. I was heavily influenced by those medical aspirations, and I graduated as a biology major in hopes of going to medical school. College was a transformative time, because I was socially and politically awakened to my Asian American/Filipino American identity. I thrived, flourished, and took a turn away from medicine. Thus, it paved the way for me to pursue a career in higher education and led me to a doctoral degree in Higher Education Leadership from Sam Houston State University.

Throughout my higher education career, I always felt compelled to lift up my own Filipino American community. I wanted other Filipino American students to know that, as an administrator, I was here to help them, and that they could pursue any career imaginable beyond the medical narrative. This led me to investigate Filipino American community college students and their stories surrounding their educational and career journey as my dissertation topic.

Our Studies

We both reflected on our studies using narrative inquiry. Collecting stories from our participants was the primary form of data. Pat Lindsay's study is titled *Kuwento/Stories: A narrative inquiry of Filipino American Community College Students*. Ricardo's study is titled *"Mexican Schools" in 1940–1950's Rural Texas: Their Impact on the College Aspirations of a Future Generation*. This section offers a brief overview of each of our studies to provide a focus on the cultural relevance of storytelling in qualitative research.

Kuwento/Stories: A narrative inquiry of Filipino American community college students

In my study, I listened to and documented kuwentos told by Filipino American community college students from the South. There were eight participants in the study; four identified as female and four identified as male. They were all under the age of 30. Most of the participants were former students of mine who attended community college at one point in their lives. Because of my good rapport with them as a college mentor, they viewed me as an *Ate*, pronounced *ah-teh*, older sister, and were comfortable sharing their kuwentos with me. Three of the participants now have careers in the medical field, and the rest are in careers outside of the medical field, including technology, real estate, aviation, and finance. The community college experience of Filipinx students used *kuwento ng mga tao*, which provided the "story of a people." The use of storytelling allowed me to create frameworks developed around personal lived experiences.

Some key themes that were developed in my study are as follows: (a) developing a Filipino American ethno-racial identity, (b) Filipino Americans in higher education settings, (c) the influence and impact of parents, family, and community, and (d) mental health issues. Participants were developing a Filipino American ethno-racial identity without even knowing it. There were several factors that influenced how they saw their Filipino American selves. Some factors were cultural influences within their own family, current pop culture, and experiences in the school setting. Filipino culture was rooted in the home and family, through food, language, traditions, customs, and community. Parents, family, and community were influential factors in selecting and navigating educational choices and career pathways. Because community college was close to home, affordable, and had strong programs in allied health such as nursing, families encouraged participants to go to community college instead of the university. Because of parental and cultural pressures, students told stories of creating a mismatch of academic and personal values within the self and others, which led to an internal and external tension. All participants confessed that their parents and relatives had told them to go into the medical industry, specifically nursing. Out of the eight participants, only one advanced to become a nurse. The rest of the participants changed their majors and career paths despite these influences.

Depending on the participants' experiences, I observed that students either developed a curiosity or disdain of self and culture. This was initiated by their learning and understanding of Filipino American history and, more evidently, the lack of knowledge of our people's existence in America. Unfortunately, with a lack of access to Asian American studies and Filipino American studies in Texas, each student has expressed the dearth of Filipino representation in their curriculum, especially for students who have degree plans that do not include mandatory classes that focus on ethnic identity. The closest place to learn and experience Filipino American identity was through Filipino American Student Associations (FSA) when they transferred to the university. Even then, participants left the FSA when they felt the organization's definition of Filipino American no longer connected with them due to FSA's heavy social agenda.

Participants also shared the lack of representation of Filipino American professionals in higher education settings, which led them to feel unsupported and isolated. One participant shared that she had a Filipina mentor at the community college, and when she transferred to a large public research university, the one Filipino staff member was not as warm or accommodating to her. Finally, stories of mental health issues described stress and anxiety associated with identity crisis. This was especially evident when it came to education and career decisions. One participant was being compared by his parents to another cousin who was successful in their education and career. With the added pressure to be successful, the participant was undergoing a crisis, as he was balancing having a parent with cancer, breaking up with his partner, and then failing pre-nursing classes he did not want to pursue. Through these kuwentos, I was able to spotlight the Filipino American experience in education and the state of higher education for students and professionals like me. I know there are more stories to uncover, understand, and share, a fact that fuels my hopes and aspirations to keep discovering my people's stories.

"Mexican Schools" in 1940s–1950s rural Texas: Their impact on the college aspirations of a future generation

In my study, I collected the stories and oral histories of Latino elders who attended segregated "Mexican schools" during the 1950s in rural areas of central Texas. The educational history of Mexican Americans in the Southwest was characterized by schools being used as instruments "of social control [with] an attempt to socialize Mexican Americans into loyal and disciplined workers" to serve white communities (Donato, 1997, p. 12). The motivation for my study stemmed from the fact that this educational history was missing in my own educational background. Knowledge of "Mexican schools" came primarily from family stories and my father's recollections of his own schooling in rural central Texas. In listening to my father's stories, one of the most startling facts about my family's educational history that I learned was that the youngest members of the community, those in elementary school, were usually the recipients of the worst outcomes of racism—bullying, mental abuse, overt hatred, and deculturalization (Black, 1997; Cameron, 2016; Rivas-Rodriguez, 2015; Spring, 2016). Despite these harsh learning conditions, former Mexican school students like my father still held idealistic notions that education could provide societal advancement for a better life in the United States (Spring, 2016).

As I became a higher education researcher, I was curious as to how former students of these segregated Mexican schools in Texas reflected on their educational aspirations, despite experiencing the harsh reality of racism at a young age. In particular, I was interested to find out if these individuals had college aspirations for themselves and if their experiences impacted the aspirations held by their own families. The purpose of my study was to bring awareness of an important area in the educational history of Latinx populations in the United States, especially for Mexican Americans. The education history of the United States has often overlooked the schooling experiences of Mexican Americans (Cameron, 2016; Donato, 1997; Rivas-Rodriguez, 2015). In my study, there were seven participants whose average age was 83.5 years.

Collectively, my participants provided 501 total years of lived experiences providing detailed insights into this scarce educational history. The collection of these narratives was valuable in creating three areas describing the segregated educational experiences of Mexican Americans during this time.

The first area is what I described as "knowing their presence," which provided detailed descriptions of the learning spaces found in these segregated schools. The second area, "hearing the experiences," provided essence descriptions which included detailed memories, actions, and emotions that occurred in a day in the life of schooling for these former students. The third area focused on how my participants, as young children, made sense of the segregation they experienced and how this influenced their college aspirations. Through their stories, I learned how past injustices faced by these elders served as motivation to "retaliate" against future educational barriers. Their stories of educational plight served as strategies to motivate the next generation of Mexican American college students. The significance of my study was that as this generation continued to age, their knowledge and insight could possibly be lost if educational leaders and researchers did not hear their voices and document their stories. This generation of voices must be heard and understood so that we do not forget this important piece of Texas and U.S. history (Cameron, 2016; Rivas-Rodriguez, 2016).

In hearing the early educational experiences of former students of one "Mexican school" in rural Central Texas, I found that these experiences had long-term influence on the educational aspirations of this generation of Mexican American learners. Determined not to have history repeat itself, the elders I spoke to for my study informed me that the stories they tell their own children, nieces, nephews, and grandchildren are strategies to build strength in the face of the systemic racism and discrimination that continues to impact the Mexican American educational experience today.

Our Reflections

We conversed about how our studies impacted us as scholars from racially minoritized communities. We felt that the stories heard in our research influenced our new scholar identities and redefined purposes of research. Our reflections were primarily focused on "data," the stories we collected from our participants. We understood that these stories were important oral histories taken from our communities. Narrative inquiry is an act of asking individuals to share stories of themselves, their lives, and their identity. One of us did research focused on a new generation of young college adult learners, and the other did research on a generation of learners whose voices are gradually leaving us. We discovered that narrative inquiry created a meaningful developmental process for our participants. We asked individuals to share stories of themselves, their lives, and their identity. For many of the participants, it was their first time speaking their stories and truths into the universe.

We chose oral storytelling as a method to reveal past and current social injustices, providing our participants with space to be heard. We realized our research process was providing empowerment and agency—to the participants and the community. Our own experiences and histories were becoming intertwined with the stories we were collecting. Some participants asked, "What are you going to do with my story?" and wondered how storytelling would expose their truths and describe their forgotten history. Another question asked by participants was "Why do you want to hear my story? I have nothing to say." I surprisingly learned that this was often said to Pat Lindsay by her community elders after she encouraged them to tell their life stories. She found out that storytelling worked as means of prompting and emboldening voices that had been suppressed and unwelcomed. For Ricardo's study, participants were willing to share with him, as a stranger, stories of their pain and triumphs as children dealing with educational disparity. Participants were willing to dig into their own memories and to recall experiences they had never before shared with anyone.

Our Use of Storytelling

After completion of our studies, we continued discussing how storytelling impacted our sense of self as researchers, but most importantly, as members of our own ethnic communities. We discovered that narrative inquiry created a meaningful developmental process for our participants. We asked individuals to share stories of themselves, their lives, and their identity. In our research, we realized the importance of generational voices in educational experiences. Pat Lindsay documented stories from a new generation of young adult college learners that will fill the gap in the community college experience for Filipinos. Ricardo documented a generation of learners whose experiences are not found in Texas history books and whose voices are gradually departing from this physical earth. We intentionally selected narrative inquiry to provide spaces for our participants to be heard. We found that oral storytelling revealed past and current social injustices. Our research process was providing empowerment and agency to our participants and the community. We identified three areas to address in our identities as qualitative researchers: knowledge creation, collective consciousness, and cultural empowerment. Under each of these areas, we created a prompt for us to contemplate in our qualitative researcher development. We constructed a composite response to our prompt providing shared ideas and guidance to further enhance our understanding of storytelling as a culturally relevant tool in qualitative research. Each composite response concludes with a *reflexion/repleksyon* describing how we used our new researcher knowledge to further advocate and assist our Filipino and Latinx communities.

Knowledge Creation

To honor our ancestral history, we must learn and know our history. A Filipino cultural proverb states: "*Ang hindi lumingon sa pinanggalingan ay hindi makakarating sa paroroonan*," which essentially translates to "For someone who does not look back, will never know where they are going." This proverb means to search for, remember, and honor your family, your culture, and your own history in order to move forward and "know where you are going." By understanding the past, we are able to understand the present and determine our future pathways. Our past stories inform who we will become as people.

Have we sincerely honored the use of kuwentos/testimonios passed down from our familial ancestors? Yes, we believe we have honored the use of kuwentos/testimonios passed down from our familial ancestors, because we are researching for the progress and representation of our own communities. In order for the Filipino American and Latinx community to be represented, acknowledged, and respected, we believe that we need to do insightful work as a Filipina and Latino looking into our own histories—past, present, and future. We must have curiosity, inspiration, motivation, and access to discover our own history. We have found that as racially minoritized researchers, we need to use our knowledge of qualitative methodologies to find and reveal our hidden histories for others to learn.

History is a subject taught from primary school to higher education, but whose kuwentos/testimonios are shared? Is it relatable or relevant to our experience? What have we heard in our own curriculums? Whose voices are represented in the research we read and share in our classes? Do the people sharing and teaching our research come from our community or from outside our community? Our research provides voices missing in the literature, and also the lack of knowledge around BIPOC communities that have been in the United States. For example, during Pat Lindsay's doctoral dissertation research, she began accumulating Filipino American history and culture articles for her literature review. She soon discovered that Filipinos have been immigrating and settling in the United States since the first documented Filipinos arrived in Morro Bay, California, in October 1587, before the first pilgrims arrived in 1620. Throughout her primary and secondary education, this history was never taught to her in school. It was only through her own research and community service in the Filipino American community that she was able to discover and learn about her history. We both agree that learning about one's history should not be found at the doctoral stage, but at the very early stages of education.

Our stories are documented and written by non-BIPOC voices that have not experienced our journey, further disrespecting and disregarding the significance of BIPOC people's stories and self-agency in telling our own narrative. There are historians, documentarians, and anthropologists who look from the outside in, and take our communities' stories for their own gain and profit, leaving the community exposed and used.

To create our knowledge, we have to excavate the past, with kuwentos/testimonios serving as a framework for understanding the current issues facing the community members we serve. Histories of colonization, genocide, and caste systems have been part of both of our communities. The more we learn about our own history, the deeper we will dig into the past, until all kuwentos/testimonios are revealed. Searching for oneself in American history unveils mixed emotions—sadness, anger, happiness, joy, and pride—knowing your community's lived experiences have made up and continue to create this country.

We need to begin with our own family histories and stories and then connect them to historical events of the past. We both realized that our family stories have rich, symbolic meanings that add additional context to any narrative inquiry studies we pursue.

Reflexion/Repleksyon.

Pat Lindsay created Leaving A Legacy: From Ideas to Published Book, a writing class with six elders aged 67 to 81, and guided them in writing and sharing their own kuwentos on a weekly basis. Over a span of several months, the elders gathered their writings, and she polished them up by creating a book cover based on their original design, edited, formatted, and printed their kuwentos. Their writings were turned into beautiful hardcover books that they could hold in their hands and give to their families. This class provided empowerment and self-authorship to document the elders' own legacy stories. Once the books were printed, Pat Lindsay and her storytellers were invited to participate in a panel workshop at the premier Filipino American National Historical Society conference in Seattle. Five of the elders proudly presented their books and encouraged other aspiring authors to write their kuwento. Writing and sharing their kuwento empowered them, and now they pass it forward and empower others to do the same.

Ricardo created the Latinx Network (LN) Writers Group within a higher education student affairs professional organization. He worked with "scholar practitioners" to create scholarship using the idea of *la familia and family stories*. In using this plan, he aimed to increase Latinx scholar practitioners from the field to add their voices in academic circles and to demystify the publication process. The LN Writers Group was founded on the idea that writing and publishing our collective knowledge provides a powerful tool to promote advocacy and empowerment for members. His goal was to create a supportive practitioner-scholar community to help others through the writing process. By way of monthly meetings, group idea sharing, and collaborative writing projects, the group became an active contributor of innovative ideas and vital scholarly research in student affairs. Ricardo's aim was to make publishing not an unattainable task, but one that is reachable to strengthen the voices of our members.

Collective Consciousness

In doing our research, we were able to create group think to create counter narratives. Our research topics offered validation to their lived experiences. In learning that others were sharing stories, our participants felt compelled to share their stories, too, where kuwentos/testimonios took root. A collective consciousness was born from group sharing and motivation. Elders and young adults were awakening to their own identity and purpose in life. In doing so, they were also remembering sometimes traumatic experiences of educational discrimination that needed to be documented in this age of removing and silencing "critical perspectives."

Has kuwentos/testimonios informed us on oppression in our communities? Yes, we believe that kuwentos/testimonios have informed us of oppression in our communities. The act of writing, sharing and documenting our stories is an act of liberation from the denial of our history in the Texas education system. From performing our studies, we realized that internalized oppression holds people back from writing and sharing their own stories. In the process of collecting kuwentos/testimonios, we heard phrases such as: "*My story isn't important,*" "*Who is going to hear my story?*" and "*I don't know where to begin.*" The internalized oppression comes from many forms of systemic oppressors telling our communities that our presence, contributions, and stories are not important and do not matter.

Reflexion/Repleksyon

We are being authentic to the stories that are shared with us—for example, when relying on difficult memories, we used the language spoken to us in our research, Taglish & Spanglish, a fusion of English with Tagalog and Spanish. This honors and respects the true voices represented in storytelling. In addition, when we forget, we rely on others who have experienced the same situations to jog our memory and hold us accountable. Kuwentos/testimonios, the stories we heard in our studies, kept us connected and intertwined in the recollections of our communities. We became aware of the emotion and pain from stories we had never heard. As we explored our unknown histories, we realized the hollow gravity of the missing pieces of our communities' stories. Our reflexive journaling in our studies often documented our tears, anger, and sadness to contextualize this oppression.

Cultural Empowerment

We also want to promote awareness of the complexities in Filipino American & Latinx culture. Filipino and Latinx experiences are multifaceted and not monolithic. The kuwentos/testimonios should be used as part of diversity, equity, and inclusion work. By finding commonalities in our ethnic cultures, we display solidarity through the intersection of our community's stories. This should be a strong foundation for working across the aisle and working together.

Have we used kuwentos/testimonios to further empower our communities? Yes, we believe we have used our narrative inquiry research experiences to empower families, colleagues, and communities. Pat Lindsay has since become a leader within the Filipino American National Historical Society–Houston, Texas chapter, a nonprofit that preserves and documents the history of Filipino Americans. She has also built upon the writing class and created a small business, Kuwento Co., that helps people contribute their life stories to a book. As founder of the LN Writers Group, Ricardo has helped Latinx colleagues to publish book chapters, newsletter articles, opinion essays, peer-reviewed articles, and one edited book documenting the Latinx experience in higher education student affairs.

Narrative inquiry is a powerful research method. We see kuwentos/testimonios as "theory in the flesh" (Latina Feminist Group, 2001). The stories found in our research are connected to living bodies. We should respect these bodies. Our people's histories, truths, and struggles are living in our blood, bodies, mind and spirit, from one generation to the infinite future. Their stories provide what is missing and not known in our textbooks, scholarly journals, and classrooms.

Reflexion/Repleksyon.

In our studies, we discovered that theater was used as a means of storytelling and empowerment—both in contemporary Filipino and Latinx communities and in the past. We are extremely interested in doing future research on this topic, one that helps us understand how cultural arts and other community activities empower individuals. Filipino festivals in the United States are a safe and consumer-friendly space for Filipino Americans and non-Filipinos to take pride in what it means to be Filipino through food, arts, history, culture, and performances. In Mexican American communities across Texas, especially in rural areas, Fiesta Patrias festivals were remembered by participants in the "Mexican school" study. At these Mexican community festivals, which still take place today, Mexican historical events are reenacted to celebrate Mexico's official independence holidays and patriotism. Through storytelling, additional context was provided on how theater performance was used to educate young children on the history missing from their schooling. We both learned through our research that cultural empowerment can be symbolically and effectively presented through the arts presented within the community.

Conclusion

In this chapter, we share our story as a Filipina and Latino who are in constant development of our scholar identities and as individuals always becoming in our ethnic identities. We see ourselves as learning from each other in the work we do in higher education and our communities. We bring to this chapter a unique relationship as qualitative research colleagues. Pat Lindsay began her doctorate as Ricardo was beginning his faculty tenure process and taught Pat Lindsay as one of her professors. Pat Lindsay invited Ricardo to serve on her dissertation committee. As she was doing her qualitative dissertation study, Ricardo was completing his own qualitative research study as part of his scholarship agenda for tenure. As researchers from diverse backgrounds, our own shared stories played an influential part in the development of this chapter.

We invite our colleagues to provide their own reflections/reflexion/repleksyon, much like we did, in doing qualitative research using storytelling. We began to understand that it is hard to remove our own lived experiences, personal theories, and common knowledge from our studies. In using storytelling in our work, we realize that stories are more than just data—they are experiences that impact our sense of self when doing research. Our participants' stories are our stories. As researchers from diverse backgrounds, our experiences and histories are intertwined with the stories we collect. We encourage our colleagues to understand the impacts and tensions that exist when doing qualitative research.

References

Black, M. S. (1997). How agrarian cultural values shaped Texas schools for Mexican children, 1910–1930. *Interchange, 28*(1), 15–30.

Cameron, D. J. (2016). The Reverend Guillermo Ibarra: A legacy of accommodation and resistance through religion and education in the Brazos Valley. *Southwestern Historical Quarterly, 49*(4), 354–376.

Donato, R. (1997). *The other struggle for equal schools: Mexican Americans during the Civil Rights Era.* SUNY Press.

Latina Feminist Group. (2001). *Telling to live: Latina feminist testimonios.* Duke University Press.

National Center for Education Statistics. (2022). Characteristics of postsecondary faculty. *Condition of Education.* U.S. Department of Education, Institute of Education Sciences. https://nces.ed.gov/programs/coe/indicator/csc.

Rivas-Rodriguez, M. (2015). *Texas Mexican Americans and postwar civil rights.* University of Texas Press.

Spring, J. (2016). *Deculturalization and the struggle for equality: A brief history of the education of dominated cultures in the United States.* Routledge.

THREE

"We Know Who We Are": A Métis Digital Storytelling Project During COVID-19

Robert Henry, Chelsea Gabel, and Amanda LaVallee

Introduction

COVID-19 HAS HAD A DETRIMENTAL impact on the daily lives of peoples globally. Governmental policies on restrictions and surveillance were implemented in an attempt to reduce the spread of the virus. For Indigenous communities (First Nations, Métis, and Inuit), early COVID-19 measures focused on community lockdowns, including checkpoints to limit individuals coming into and out of their communities, gathering restrictions, and the temporary closure of community facilities (Richmond et al., 2020). The public health restrictions put in place by governments and communities impacted research programs, as many were put on hold or suspended in compliance with COVID-19 restrictions. Of all research approaches, qualitative research programs—specifically community-engaged research projects—faced the greatest impact from university research ethics boards, which created ad hoc policies to abide by ever-shifting public health measures.[1]

In Canada, research ethics are framed by the Tri-Council Policy Statement 2 (TCPS 2), wherein research is to be designed to cause the least amount of harm within a community.[2] Due to the negative history of research in and on Indigenous peoples, national research ethics boards have created specific research protocols for researchers to follow. Chapter 9 of the TCPS 2 herein focuses specifically on research with Indigenous communities, where there is a greater level of risk assessment to make sure that research is done in a good way, adheres to OCAP™ [3] (ownership, access, control and possession) Principles for research with Indigenous communities and organizations, and follows community protocols.[4] As COVID-19 continues, community-engaged scholars must find ways to alter their research methods to try to adhere to community realities and shifting research ethics policies. Most researchers, community partners, and participants have looked to online platforms such as Zoom to conduct qualitative research, specifically interviews and focus groups. For Indigenous community-engaged research, the switch to online engagement was met at times with cynicism, as online platforms were seen to limit relational accountability, the foundation of Indigenous research paradigms (Chilisa, 2019; Henry et al., 2016; Kovach, 2021; Wilson, 2008) and integral to arts-based research methods (Henry & Gabel, 2019). However, despite the barriers and shifts to accommodate COVID-19 public health protocols, Indigenous community-engaged researchers have been able to pivot and continue their research programs and projects.

This chapter focuses on how the experiences of a Métis community-engaged digital storytelling research project that explores Métis identity shifted its approach to comply with research protocols brought about by COVID-19. Our contribution to this special collection is divided into four sections. First, we provide background information about the importance of the project and who the Métis peoples are. Second, we lay out the broad principles of arts-based research with a focus on digital storytelling methodology. Third, we examine how the community-engaged project pivoted to an online format due to COVID-19 restrictions put in place through university policies. Here we draw on participant narratives to show that, despite moving to an online format, a strong sense of community was developed between participants and researchers, highlighting that relationality (Wilson, 2008; Henry et al., 2016; Chilisa, 2019) can be achieved through an online platform. The fourth and final section provides lessons learned and considerations for other researchers who are looking to engage in an online, community-engaged, arts-based approach with Métis and, more broadly, Indigenous communities. Based on our sound methodology, carefully adapted methods, and conscious attention to and communication with community members and participants, we found that despite initial challenges related to shifting Indigenous research practices to an online environment, a relational connection and sense of community can be accomplished.

Métis Peoples, Politics, and Identity in Canada

Who the Métis are and what it means to be Métis are politically charged questions in Canada (Macdougall, 2011; Andersen, 2014; Gaudry and Leroux, 2017;

Teillet, 2019). Métis peoples are one of three distinct Indigenous peoples in Canada and have unique identity, values, language, and cultural traditions that distinguish them from the other two Indigenous groups (First Nations and Inuit). However, the Canadian government did not recognize Métis as Indigenous peoples until the Constitution Act of 1982 (Canadian Charter of Rights and Freedoms, 1982). Since the Constitution Act, the term Métis has gained significant usage across Canada, but the definition of who Métis persons are has varied over time and place. Unfortunately, there are competing definitions in existence today that create political dissension over funding Métis peoples, communities, and organizations, as well as national, provincial, and community dubiety and discomfiture regarding who we are. This is due in part to the misunderstanding that anyone with some Indigenous and European ancestry is then, automatically, Métis. In 2002, the Métis National Council General Assembly adopted the following national definition: "'Métis' means a person who self identifies as Métis, is distinct from other Aboriginal peoples, is of historic Métis Nation Ancestry, and is accepted by the Métis Nation" (Métis National Council, 2022). Andersen (2014) notes that Métis have typically been misrecognized as mixed-descent and mixed-"race" identity, rather than a political and historically coherent Indigenous people. He states that the problem with using a mixed-raced understanding of "Métis" is that it finds "Métis" everywhere, and in so doing denies the more explicit peoplehood of the Métis Nation. Gaudry (2018) also critiques the prevalent discourse around Métis identity and the increasing number of "newly self-identifying Métis" (p. 164). For example, due to the ready availability of DNA ancestry testing kits, there are concerns about the increasing number of self-identifying Métis people in Eastern Canada (Andersen, 2014; Gaudry & Leroux, 2017; Leroux, 2018). However, having a mix of European and Indigenous ancestry is *not* Métis; rather, Métis people and identity is connected to a specific culture, land, kinship, and history (Macdougall, 2011; Andersen, 2014; Isaac, 2016).

Métis peoplehood and nationhood have shaped Métis relations pre- and post-development of Canada as a country—for example, through their relationships to the fur trade, developing an economic system with First Nations and incoming settlers (i.e., pemmican trade) (Royal Commission on Aboriginal Peoples [RCAP], 1996), politically through the development of the Manitoba Act, the creation of longstanding settlements (i.e., the Alberta settlements and communities in northern Saskatchewan), and military protectionism (i.e., Red River and the Northwest Resistances). However, Euro-Canadian policies have been effective in pushing Métis peoples into the margins of Canadian society. For example, after the Northwest Resistance of 1885, the Métis became a forgotten people, cast aside as settlers began to move west in larger and larger droves and to control the land, creating a diaspora effect (Andersen, 2014; Teillet, 2019). In exchange for Metis land rights, the Canada government created the scrip system, whereby land or equivalent dollar values were offered to Métis (Teillet, 2019). For Métis, the dispossession from their lands through the often coercive and fraudulent scrip system, and the subsequent forced surrender of their Indigenous title in the west, dislocated communities and fragmented Métis families (Dorion & Prefontaine, 2001). While some families maintained their ties and pride in their Métis roots, other Métis families decided to move underground or to hide their identity or connection to their Métis identities (Desmarais, 2013). Those who could, would deny their heritage and became assimilated into the Euro-Canadian mainstream to escape negative stereotypes and continuing economic hardship (Sealey & Lussier, 1975; Teillet, 2019).

Despite the ongoing attacks on their peoplehood and nation, Métis have persevered and achieved a cultural reawakening that began in the late 1940s when Métis political and educational organizations began to sprout up across the nation to provide Métis-specific educational and cultural programs (Teillet, 2019). Métis began to mobilize themselves again to protect their livelihoods and assert their presence in communities through the development of Métis locals, i.e., chartered communities (Graham & Davoren, 2015). Since 1982, following the recognition of Métis as Aboriginal Peoples in the Canadian Constitution Act, the Métis National Council was established to represent Métis people and communities nationally and to align provincial Métis governments, first with Alberta, Saskatchewan, and Manitoba, and later Ontario and British Columbia (Welch, 2023).

It was not until mid-1980 that there began to be an increase in those claiming to be Métis or connected to a Métis community. At the time, Métis began to receive provincial and federal financial support for education, as well as hunting and harvesting rights (Dubois & Saunders, 2013). According to Statistics Canada, Métis people represented just over 35% of the total Indigenous population in 2016, an increase of 51.2% over 2006 (Statistics Canada, 2018).

This increase is larger than First Nations and Inuit, which also saw a modest population increase. Much of the increase is attributed to the various programs and services that have been accrued by Métis governments for their citizens, which include employment assistance services, skills training and education, financial support enabling program participation, first-time home purchase loans, and undergraduate and graduate scholarships (Métis Nation Saskatchewan). With the increase of programs and access to education, as well as cultural shifts (where being Métis became less shameful) and institutional equity hiring policies, there has been an increase in non-Indigenous peoples claiming connection to Métis identity and communities. Most recently, it has been within universities that high-profile cases have resulted in a spotlight being shone on Métis identity (Leo, 2021; Tait & Henry, 2022). As a result of the history of erasure of Métis people from Canada to their recent inclusion, to the increase in economic opportunities, Métis citizens are still being erased from their own experiences. Because of the limited understandings of Métis, even within Indigenous spaces, Métis voices continue to be silenced within research, as data and projects focus on self-identification and not on citizenship. By and large, academics, Métis, and non-Métis have explored Métis experiences centering on historical, archival, and census data (Andersen, 2014; Gaudry, 2014; Macdougall, 2011). While these approaches help to contextualize Métis peoples in a located time and place to validate Métis presence, they do not provide opportunities for Métis people to talk about what it means to be Métis today. Thus, there is a strong need for research in Métis communities from a Métis perspective.

It is from this space that the project "*We know who we are: Intergenerational understandings of Métis identity and well-being using digital storytelling*" was developed. This project explores the ways in which Métis Elders, adults, and youth have come to understand their identity. Specifically, it looks at how intergenerational relationships shape Métis identity, and how these relationships currently influence the health and well-being of Métis people through a community-engaged, arts-based, digital storytelling approach. The following project is offered to demonstrate the sorts of community-engaged, online tensions we experienced. We will not be presenting "research results" as such, but methodological detail.

Arts-Based Research and the Digital Storytelling Methodology

Arts-based genres in qualitative research have flourished over the last few decades and have generated rich data from their application (Castleden, Garvin, & Huu-ay-aht First Nation, 2008; Henry & Gabel, 2019; Poudrier & Thomas-MacLean, 2009). Arts-based methods assist in shifting the power differential between researcher and participant to create a positive space for the cocreation of knowledge (Gabel & LaVallee, 2023; Henry & Gabel, 2019). The data co-created is valued for being rich, descriptive, and robust, leading to more opportunities to engage in knowledge translation and mobilization outcomes that benefit the community (de Jager et al., 2017). Additionally, community-engaged participatory research has become a desired approach within Indigenous health and social realms to aid in understanding the dynamic and multifaceted issues leading to community-led solutions (Unger, 2019). Historically, Indigenous peoples have been "researched to death" (Smith, 2021). Thus, community-engaged participatory research helps to create bridges between researchers and communities using shared knowledge and experiences. It further establishes a mutual trust that enhances both the quality and quantity of data collected. The key benefit from these collaborations is a deeper understanding of a community's unique circumstances and a more accurate framework for adapting "good practices" to the community's needs (Unger, 2019).

Digital storytelling (DST) has gained popularity recently as an arts-based participatory research method for capturing stories of community members (Lambert & Hessler, 2018). Stories shared by community members about their pressing health and social issues are valued sources of information for health and social providers and policymakers (Lambert & Hessler, 2018). The uses of DST range from creative expression to a research method for exploring community health issues and needs. Moreover, others use it for sharing family moments, preserving oral history, and reflective learning in the classroom. DST takes the listener or reader on an exploration into deeper understanding (Lambert, 2010).

DST was developed in the early 1990s by Joe Lambert and Dana Atchley at the Centre for Digital Storytelling (now called the StoryCenter[5]) in Berkeley, California. Digital stories are three- to five-minute films using text, music, art, still images, and voiceover to document participant understandings of the research questions. DST is a creative activity wherein those involved have the opportunity to talk about their knowledge, experiences, and perceptions regarding a topic, while acquiring skills in short filmmaking. The StoryCenter uses a specific process for facilitating DST workshops, whereby a typical workshop is organized over three days for a total of 21 hours of instruction. Throughout these three days, participants create a 250-to 375-word script, with 12–15 images or small video clips to help in the visualization of their script. These workshops have experienced facilitators guiding the group, and although the creation of a DST is an individual expression, the workshops are collaborative, inclusive, and supportive, and all in attendance help to shape each other's DST (Lambert & Hessler, 2018). Many people trained in DST often use an adaptation of the model developed by the StoryCenter (Lambert, 2010).

In 2019, the research team (Gabel, Henry, and LaVallee) attended an in-person DST workshop at the StoryCenter in Berkeley, California, to acquire training to lead DST workshops with our participants. DST was the chosen research methodology because it can be used as an independent research method or combined with other methods. Moreover, through a Métis research framework, DST is a respectful, relevant, reciprocal, and responsible method grounded in ethics of relational accountability and is complementary to Indigenous approaches to research (Gabel & LaVallee, forthcoming). Relational accountability holds researchers responsible to participants as well as their communities, thus maintaining a respectful and mutually beneficial relationship throughout and beyond the research (Kovach, 2021; Wilson, 2008). This method aligns with Indigenous methodologies, as many Indigenous (First Nation, Métis, Inuit) Peoples' traditional knowledge transmission is based on oral tradition. Oral tradition is both informal and formal storytelling that communicates the histories, values, lessons, morals, and worldviews to the family and community and provides connections among people. It is the connections across space, place, and time that bind together Indigenous culture, history, and values (Iseke, 2013; Kovach, 2021; Wilson, 2008).

Methodological Adaptations

Prior to COVID-19, our research plan was to bring 12–15 participants together to attend a three-day workshop hosted by the StoryCentre in Saskatoon, Saskatchewan, in the fall of 2020. However, as a research team in the midst of COVID-19, we required a reflexive approach that allowed us to be open to the necessary methodological adaptions, given the complexity of our relational methodology and the unpredictable elements of online research processes. There were both possibilities and limitations to these adaptations. Although we had originally planned for our DST workshops to be facilitated in-person, we decided to shift them to synchronous online sessions. As such, we made significant adaptations to the DST workshop method. To move online, the research team worked with the StoryCenter to develop a workshop process that consisted of all the necessary teachings and sharing about the DST method and technology, as well as creating a Métis relational online space to share our stories. As such we developed one-day-a-week, two-hour online DST workshop sessions, which consisted of a total of 12 hours over a six-week period, compared to a three-day, in-person workshop of 21 hours. This meant that considerable time was spent with participants outside of the set workshop timeframe to allow for a relational connection, as well as DST method and technological support.

With the shift to an online platform, the research team developed a process to support participants, as well as to try to build a space of relational accountability. Therefore, prior to the workshops, participants were contacted by telephone and online to allow time to share stories of who they are and where they come from (family, community, land), as well as their experiences, motivations, and interests (knowledge and teachings). We furthered this contact with follow-up conversations to share about the intentions of the project, review ethics, and conduct a pre-interview with semi-structured questions. The semi-structured questions were designed to have participants begin constructing their personal stories, as well as to talk about their perceptions about Métis identity, culture, and well-being.

Once pre-workshop interviews were completed, participants were provided with technological support around online conferencing (Zoom) and technological software used by the StoryCenter (WeVideo). The first workshop was an information session that involved StoryCenter facilitators introducing themselves and the DST method. Time was provided for participants to introduce themselves and sharing who they are, where they are from, family name, community connections, and intentions for the workshop. This session was important, as it provided an opportunity for participants to get to know others and build relationships. For example, some participants found out that they shared similar family names and were distantly related. As one participant noted, "The social aspect of this process was my favorite part. It was incredible being able to connect with folks from across the Prairies and hear about their families, lives and stories."

The final methodological additions were twofold and involved a digital story screening and celebration, wherein participants viewed each other's stories. This was followed by a kitchen table talk. (Traditionally, Métis peoples engaged in daily life that centered around the kitchen table.) These activities included visiting with friends and relatives, storytelling and story listening, discussing politics, playing cards, dancing, playing music, eating, and drinking. The kitchen table approach, i.e., a small, informal meeting that takes place in someone's home or a local coffee shop, is used in research to enable dialogue that is informal, relaxed, and consistent with Métis ways of knowing and doing (Davey, 2017). This format of gathering stories in a group setting is beneficial because it encourages interaction between participants, which helps to generate conversation and identify group norms. The kitchen table approach and method was used throughout the six-week process and also at the end of the workshop in lieu of a focus group to discuss each other's digital stories. One participant highlighted the importance of the kitchen table in their story, and the significance it had on their learning from older people when they were younger.

> My favourite part was hearing the stories and experiences of other participants. We had many places and experiences in common, which made the meetings feel comfortable. It made me realize that the prairie Métis community is a relatively small group of people with common history and culture. I felt great respect for the process other participants worked through. It felt like a safe space to share personal history.

As a methodology, kitchen table talks brought participants together in a culturally specific way that highlighted an intergenerational process of learning.

Lessons Learned

Indigenous research has a strong connection to relational accountability (Chilisa, 2019; Kovach, 2021; Wilson, 2008). Given the shifting health policies, qualitative research had to adjust, and there was hesitation on the part of the research team to move the digital storytelling project to an online format, because it was feared that a community-engaged approach and relational accountability would not be able to be maintained through an online delivery. A second issue of concern was the ability to provide the necessary support to participants, because of the varied levels of digital literacy. For example, one participant did not have a computer but attended all meetings via their phone. Other concerns related to digital literacy included trouble with software application—both the online platform and digital story software. The Elder participants required increased support in learning how to use basic functions on their computers/tablets. Although we provided as much support as we could to address these concerns, other issues would arise at times due to poor connectivity and poor computer speeds when running software. However, as we moved through the project, other issues arose that researchers should take into consideration when considering moving digital storytelling to an online format.

Aside from issues related to digital technologies, time became a concern. As participants and researchers, we were spread across three different time zones, and the majority were employed or attending university, so finding a time that fit everyone's schedule was difficult. Because the digital storytelling workshop format endorsed by the StoryCenter is usually done in three-day, in-person workshops, participants can block out those days and times. However, finding a designated time that would allow individuals to participate together became difficult. The issue of time also went beyond finding a time to meet. Time was also a factor related to building relationships in a good way. To address these issues, we engaged in pre-workshop interviews with participants to help them understand the project and digital storytelling process. Here, participants would work with the research team and StoryCenter facilitators in the creation of their stories on their own time.

The second consideration relates to communication. Because participants often worked in isolation from the other participants (other than the two-hour weekly online meetings), frequent communication was vital to keeping participants on track to finish their digital stories. However, as the project moved forward, frequent communication was important to support the mental health of the research team and participants. To ensure accessible communication, we, the project team, made ourselves available to all participants at all times.

Participants were able to meet with the team outside of the workshop hours in ways not restricted to technical support. These meetings provided participants with an opportunity to tell their stories in more detail, expanding on the importance of words, phrases, and photographs that they were looking to include. For example, one participant noted how "The most challenging part of this experience was narrowing down my story. It was hard for me to pick one piece to tell." Some stories focused on themes of trauma and abuse, and therefore required extra time, guidance, and care. Additionally, the research team helped write out scripts, and helped participants choose music and photos to use within their DST. The transition to online meant that we had to create a built-in network of individuals who could assist with technical support, as well as being a listening ear as participants shared their experiences of being Métis.

Finally, as the project researchers, we recognized that some participants experienced "Zoom fatigue," which involves the tiredness, worry, or burnout associated with overusing virtual platforms of communication (Bilodeau et al., 2021). It was recommended to participants to turn their cameras off if they began to feel anxious, tired, frustrated, or needed a break from seeing themselves online. We also dedicated short breaks within our virtual meetings to allow participants to get up and move around. Further, some participants were also tired and emotionally spent from watching the final DST screenings and then participating in a kitchen table discussion. In hindsight, creating a separate time to have the kitchen table talk may have reduced the pressure on some to participate in online discussions, thus allowing for more in-depth sharing.

Conducting a Métis community-engaged research project in a synchronous online format sometimes made it challenging for individuals to connect on a personal and cultural level. We worked diligently to allow for meaningful interactions built on the 4Rs of relationality—respect, relevance, reciprocity, and responsibility (Chilisa, 2019; Henry et al., 2016; Kirkness & Barnhardt, 1991; Wilson, 2008)—interacting in a way that allowed ourselves and participants to build genuine and meaningful relationships. As Métis peoples, we understand and believe that relationships are a vital part of research. Relationships are essential because they allow for the transfer of knowledge between individuals and generations (Gaudet, 2018; LaVallee et al., 2016). One participant expressed the importance of relationality and sharing through an online format, where:

I found this process was a very reflexive/reflective experience for me as I continue to understand what it means to be Métis as a young woman who grew up disconnected from her homeland and family. Not only did I learn a lot about myself but about other Métis experiences across the West.

Despite distances and not being able to meet face-to-face, it was still possible to create a space of relationality and the importance of opening up to share and were highlighted by participants as important pillars to frame the research.

Our research centered on relational trust and establishing a virtual community that was deeply rooted in a sense of connection, where storytelling enabled us to build on the logics of Métis kinship. We created our online space to encourage active listening, which is being intentionally open and receptive to what is emerging in the present moment. Active listening created an environment where our participants felt seen and valued. As one participant noted:

> While I enjoyed creating my digital story, my favourite part of the digital storytelling process was feeling like I was part of a little community. I enjoyed getting to know everyone and learning about their stories and being amongst a group of people that understood the nuances associated with Métis identity.

Storytelling and story listening are embedded within our culture. Sharing stories virtually does not lessen the impact of that story. Therefore, story sharing helped us to create community and enabled us to see through the eyes of others and open us to the claims of others.

Moving to an online platform had numerous benefits; however, in the end, an in-person workshop was the most desirable for our participants. In our post-workshop survey, one participant noted: "If I could wish for one thing it would be that we could meet together, in person, to share our stories with each other in person." Another stated: "I think the only thing that would've improved this experience is if it could've happened in person." Overall, community-engaged online research involved a unique workload and similar in-person time commitments from the research team for the project to be successful.

Conclusion

The COVID-19 pandemic has disrupted qualitative research; however, new opportunities for researchers have emerged to enhance online research. The online adaptations were beneficial to this project, as it provided a larger geographical space for individuals to be recruited in a short amount of time. Additionally, it permitted participation on the part of those who would have difficulty in travelling and time commitment, which limited the total costs of the project. The money saved could then be used to allow more participants to attend conferences and community events to talk about their stories and experiences.

Intergenerational storytelling provides a platform for our Elders to share stories with the broader community, specifically the younger generations. Lambert and Hessler (2018) state that "identity and diversity are natural topics for storytelling as stories provide ways to address these at times complicated issues by connecting and negotiating similarities and differences" (p. 146). Digital storytelling can be a culturally relevant research tool and is congruent with Indigenous ways of knowing, as images and stories continue to be ways of sharing and expressing knowledge. As Macdougall (2017) shares about the importance of intergenerational stories and kinship: "Métis identities are nurtured and sustained by the stories, traditions and cultural practices taught by our grandmothers, grandfathers, and ancestors" (p. 5). Most importantly, digital storytelling was a form of creative expression that privileged Métis ways of knowing, centering local Métis knowledge and experience at all stages. Through a model of relationality embedded within Métis principles of sharing, we were able to successfully adapt digital storytelling within an online format. It was through these moments of sharing our lives, our customs, and our culture that allowed us to engage in Métis ways of kinship through digital and online technologies, thus highlighting that it is not so much the medium upon which relationships are built, but the ethical care dedicated to engaged logics of Métis kinship.

Notes

1. Robert Henry sat on the Behavioural Research Ethics Board at the University of Saskatchewan from 2019 to 2022 and was required to support researchers in reshaping their research projects to conform to community and university COVID-19 health policies.

2. Research involving the First Nations, Inuit, and Métis peoples of Canada. In: *Tri-Council policy statement: Ethical conduct for research involving humans* (Ottawa: Secretariat on Responsible Conduct of Research, 2014). Available at https://ethics.gc.ca/eng/documents/tcps2-2018-en-interactive-final.pdf

3. First Nations Information Governance Centre. The First Nations Principles of OCAP™ (ownership, control, access, and possession).
4. TCPS2
5. https://www.storycenter.org/

References

Andersen, C. (2014). *"Métis": Race, recognition, and the struggle for Indigenous peoplehood*. University of British Columbia Press.

Bilodeau, H., Kehler, A., & Minnema, N. *Statistics Canada. Internet use and COVID-19: How the pandemic increased the amount of time Canadians spend online*. Updated 24 June 2021. [online]. Available at https://www150.statcan.gc.ca/n1/pub/45-28-0001/2021001/article/00027-eng.htm [Accessed 22 May 2022].

Canadian Charter of Rights and Freedoms, Part 2 of the Constitution Act, 1982, being Schedule B to the Canada Act 1982 (UK), 1982, c 11.

Castleden, H., Garvin, T., & Huu-ay-aht First Nation. (2008). Modifying photovoice for community-based participatory Indigenous research. *Social science & medicine*, 66(6), 1393–1405.

Chilisa, B. (2019). *Indigenous research methodologies*. Sage.

Davey, D. (2017). *Kiya waneekah: (don't forget)*. University of Manitoba, Master's thesis.

de Jager, A., Fogarty, A., Tewson, A., Lenette, C., & Boydell, K. M. (2017). Digital storytelling in research: A systematic review. *The Qualitative Report*, 22(10), 2548–2582. https://doi.org/10.46743/2160-3715/2017.2970

Desmarais, D. A. (2013). *Colonialism's impact on the health of Métis elderly: History, oppression, identity, and consequences*. Doctoral dissertation, University of Regina.

Dorion, L., & Prefontaine, D. (2001). Deconstructing Métis historiography: Giving voice to the Métis people. In L. Barkwell, L. Dorion, & D. Prefontaine (Eds.), *Métis legacy: A Métis historiography and annotated bibliography* (pp. 13–36). Winnipeg, MB: Pemmican Publications.

Dubois, J. & Saunders, K. (2013). "Just do it!": Carving out a space for the Métis in Canadian federalism. *Canadian Journal of Political Science*, 46(1), 187–214.

Gabel, C., & LaVallee, A. (2023). "Valuing Métis identity in the prairies through a "5 R" lens: Our digital storytelling journey." Accepted in the edited collection *Strong Métis women academics: Our contributions* (University of Manitoba Press), editors: Laura Forsythe & Jennifer Markides. Publication Release Spring 2023.

Gaudet, J. C. (2018). Keeoukaywin: the visiting way—Fostering an indigenous research methodology. *Aboriginal Policy Studies*, 7(2).

Gaudry, A. (2014). Métis in Canada: History, identity, law, and politics. *Aboriginal Policy Studies*, 3(1 & 2), 231–237.

Gaudry, A. (2018). Communing with the dead: The "New Métis," Métis identity appropriation, and the displacement of living Métis culture. *American Indian Quarterly*, 42(2), 162–190. https://www.muse.jhu.edu/article/693376

Gaudry, A., & Leroux, D. (2017). White settler revisionism and making Métis everywhere: The evocation of Métissage in Quebec and Nova Scotia. *Critical Ethnic Studies*, 3(1), 116–142.

Graham, C., & Davoren, T. (2015). *Sharing their stories: Narratives of young Métis parents and elders about parenting*. Prince George, BC: National Collaborating Centre for Aboriginal Health.

Henry, R., & Gabel, C. (2019). "It's not just a picture when lives are at stake: Ethical considerations and photovoice methods with Indigenous peoples engaged in street lifestyles." *Journal of Educational Thought*, Volume 53(3): 229–260. https://journalhosting.ucalgary.ca/index.php/jet/article/view/69723

Henry, R., Tait, C., & STR8 UP. (2016). Creating ethical research partnerships–relational accountability in action. *Engaged Scholar Journal: Community-Engaged Research, Teaching, and Learning*, 2(1), 183–204.

Isaac, T. (2016). *A matter of national and constitutional import: Report of the Minister's special representative on reconciliation with Métis: Section 35 Métis rights and the Manitoba Métis Federation Decision*. https://www.aadnc-aandc.gc.ca/DAM/DAM-INTER-HQ-AI/STAGING/texte-text/report_reconciliation_1471371154433_eng.pdf

Iseke, J. (2013). Indigenous storytelling as research. *International Review of Qualitative Research*, 6, 559–577. 10.1525/irqr.2013.6.4.559.

Kirkness, V. J., & Barnhardt, R. (1991). First Nations and higher education: The four R's—Respect, relevance, reciprocity, responsibility. *Journal of American Indian Education*, 1–15.

Kovach, M. (2021). *Indigenous methodologies: Characteristics, conversations, and contexts*. University of Toronto Press.

Lambert, J. (2010). *Digital storytelling cookbook*. Berkeley, CA: Digital Diner Press. Retrieved from http://www.storycenter.org/cookbook.pdf

Lambert, J., & Hessler, B. (2018). *Digital storytelling: Capturing lives, creating community* (5th ed.). Routledge.

LaVallee, A., Troupe, C., & Turner, T. (2016). Negotiating and exploring relationships in Métis community-based research. *Engaged Scholar Journal: Community-Engaged Research, Teaching, and Learning*, 2(1), 167–182.

Leo, G. (2021). "Indigenous or Pretender." CBC News, October 27, 2021. https://www.cbc.ca/newsinteractives/features/carrie-bourassa-indigenous

Leroux, D. (2018). "We've been here for 2,000 years": White settlers, Native American DNA and the phenomenon of indigenization. *Social Studies of Science*, 48(1), 80–100.

Macdougall, B. (2011). *One of the family: Métis culture in nineteenth-century northwestern Saskatchewan*. UBC Press.

Macdougall, B. (2017). *Land, family and identity: Contextualizing Métis health and well-being*. Prince George, BC: National Collaborating Centre for Aboriginal Health.

Métis Centre of the National Aboriginal Health Organization. (2011). *Paucity of Métis-specific health and well-being data and information: Underlying Factors*. Ottawa, ON, 1–6.

Métis Nation Saskatchewan. Available at: https://Métisnationsk.com/

Métis National Council. Citizenship. Available at: https://www.Métisnation.ca/about/citizenship. Accessed August 18, 2022.

Poudrier, J. & Mac-Lean, R.T. (2009). We've fallen into the cracks": Aboriginal women's experiences with breast cancer through photovoice. *Nursing Inquiry*, 16(4), 306–317.

Richmond, C., Castleden, H., & Gabel, C. (2021). Practicing self-determination to protect Indigenous health in COVID-19: Lessons for this pandemic and similar futures. In Andrews, G. J., Crooks, V. A., Pearce, J. R., Messina, J. P. (Eds.), *COVID-19 and similar futures. Global perspectives on health geography*. Springer, Cham. https://doi.org/10.1007/978-3-030-70179-6_40

Royal Commission on Aboriginal Peoples. (1996). *Report of the Royal Commission on Aboriginal Peoples*. Ottawa: Minister of Supply and Services. https://www.bac-lac.gc.ca/eng/discover/aboriginal-heritage/royal-commission-aboriginal-peoples/Pages/final-report.aspx

Sealey, D. B., & Lussier, A. S. (1975). *The Metis: Canada's Forgotten People*. Manitoba Métis Federation Press

Smith, L. T. (2021). *Decolonizing methodologies: Research and indigenous peoples*. Bloomsbury Publishing.

Statistics Canada. (2018). *Aboriginal Peoples in Canada: Key Results from the 2016 Census*. Available at https://www150.statcan.gc.ca/n1/daily-quotidien/171025/dq171025a-eng.htm?indid=14430-3&indgeo=0

Tait, C. & Henry, R. (2023). Indigenous identity fraud: An interview with Caroline Tait. *aboriginal policy studies, 10*(2), 84–92.

Teillet, J. (2019). *The north-west is our mother: The story of Louis Riel's people, the Métis nation*. HarperCollins.

Unger, H. (2019). Community-based participatory health research: Principles and practice. *European Journal of Public Health, 29*, supp. 4, ckz185.762, https://doi.org/10.1093/eurpub/ckz185.762

Welch, M.A. (2023). Métis National Council. *The Canadian Encyclopedia*. https://www.thecanadianencyclopedia.ca/en/article/metis-national-council

Wilson, S. (2008). *Research is ceremony: Indigenous research methods*. Fernwood Publishing.

FOUR

With My Ancestors in My Studio: Re-searching My Taíno Roots

Leslie C. Sotomayor II

A Visual Journey

IN THIS CHAPTER, I REFLECT on and share my journey as I have gone back through my memories and history to unpack my own cultural identity and understanding about my paternal lineage through my abuela, Elba, a Taína from Utuado, Puerto Rico. My journey is centered on an unlearning inquisitive lens that is interwoven with colonial trauma. I intentionally engaged in this creative journey as a process of healing my own psyche and spiritual wounds. I am simultaneously the artist, the curadora, and the re-searcher. My re-search of my heritage led me to a deeper understanding of my cultural and spiritual Taíno roots and my family history through my art studio practice and autohistoria-teoría (theorizing of self) through the feminist writing practice of visual pláticas/testimonios (Sotomayor & Sperry García, 2023). Although my theorizing is anchored foundationally on Gloria Anzaldúa's writings, I am constantly in conversation with all that I glean from her and my own lived experiences as a form of spirituality that is constantly evolving, depending on where I am positioned on the spiral of life and conocimiento. In what follows, I share my paintings and visual plática/testimonio, interwoven with contextualization of my theorizing these fragments of my experiences as ongoing. I define visual pláticas and testimonios as the creative feminist practice of visual text and imagery on paper or Word document as a visual expression that may integrate imagery, letters, fonts, color, symbols or anything that the author deems necessary on the page. Creative acts: I define the creative acts as deep, meaningful, embodied experiences that are woven into our mind, body, soul, and spirit manifesting through a creative vessel. For example, painting, music, writing, dance I consider as some forms of creative acts.

Theorizing the In/Between

Anzaldúa theorizes the native Nahuatl word and meaning of nepantla at length when discussing the transformational recursive stages of conocimiento. Nepantla, a *Nahuatl* word from the native southern Mexican people meaning the "space between two bodies of water, the space between two worlds" (Anzaldúa & Keating, 2015, p. 237). Nepantla is a tumultuous place that is in transition as one transforms. Nepantla, being the second stage in the conocimiento process, occurs after a shock, *a susto*, (fear) shakes you down to your core.[1] It is only then that "éste arrebato, the earthquake, jerks you from the familiar and safe terrain and catapults you into nepantla, the second stage" (Anzaldúa & Keating, 2015, p. 122). When a person is in the process of crossing from one physical, geographical, emotional, or spiritual location into another, the crossing creates an in-between space, a gap. In the in-between space of nepantla, many things may be experienced: healing, awakening of the consciousness, acceptance of self, negotiations and contradictions. In nepantla, a person may choose to become a nepantlera, a spiritual activist as "agents of awakening, inspire and challenge others to deeper awareness, greater *conocimiento*; they serve as reminders of each other's search for wholeness of being" (Anzaldúa 1990, p. 293). It is important to note that the seven transformative recursive stages as theorized by Anzaldúa (2015) are not static or lineal, but rather fluid, and "all seven are present within each stage, they occur concurrently, chronologically or not" (Anzaldúa & Keating, 2015, p. 124). The transformational recursive stages "zigzag" through the stages with no discrimination as to time, and no exclusivity to one stage, but rather crossing in-between more than one at all times.

Conocimiento is a key characteristic of autohistoria-teoría. I refer to Anzaldúa's conocimiento theory as "transformative acts" because, in my experience, her theory evokes deep reflections that intensify when engaged, changing *something* within us. I describe the "acts" that comprise Anzaldúa's theory of conocimiento as "transformative," because each act is intended to bring about and/or to shed light on something. I also use the phrase "transformative acts" to avoid reproducing an ideology of hierarchy, as the use of steps or stages would suggest.

In bridging historical contexts, myths/religion, and re-imagining through critical reflection, creativity, and spirituality, autohistoria-teoría makes possible the rewriting of oneself. Anzaldúa states that by connecting and theorizing personal experiences with social realities and "by making certain personal experiences the subject of this study, I also blur the private/public borders" (Anzaldúa, 2015, p. 6). Through the process of connecting and theorizing personal experiences, autohistoria-teoría is "fused" together, facilitating a re-construction of oneself through agency. Anzaldúa (2015) critically engages with the concept of conocimiento as a form of resistance to traditional modes of knowing. She also refers to conocimiento as her lived practice of spiritual inquiry. For Anzaldúa, "spirituality is a symbology system.... Through spirituality we seek balance and harmony with our environment" (2015, pp. 38–39). Conocimiento, as spiritual inquiry, is "driven by the desire to understand, know, *y saber* [and know] how human and other beings know. Beneath your desire for knowledge writhes the hunger to understand and love yourself" (Anzaldúa & Keating, 2015, p. 121).

People of color (POC) or underrepresented populations who have a strong sense of not belonging and feeling in-between in their scholarship, research, or in higher education (Strayhorn, 2012), can bridge their experiences through Gloria Anzaldúa's theories of conocimiento and autohistoria-teoría.

I claim that the performative feminist writing practice of autohistoria-teoría coined by Anzaldúa (2015) is a way to create self-knowledge and belonging, and to bridge collaborative spaces through curating, education, and art. In her 2002 essay "now let us shift . . . the path of conocimiento . . . inner works . . . public acts," Anzaldúa offers the beginnings of a definition:

> Autohistoria is a term I use to describe the genre of writing about one's personal and collective history using fictive elements, a sort of fictionalized autobiography or memoir: and autohistoria-teoría, is a personal essay that theorizes. (Anzaldúa, 2009, 578)

In this vein, autohistoria-teoría is a way to create personal meaning and also to bridge collaborative work with others, as they are the reader but also make meaning of their own experiences, historical contexts, and performances (writing, art, curating, educating, etc.). In making meaning for oneself, community is also being effected through public acts initiating social change. Only when we send "our voices, visuals and visions outward into the world, we alter the walls and make them a framework for new windows and door" (Anzaldúa,

1990, p. xxv). An example of Anzaldúa's autohistoria is *La Prieta* (Anzaldúa & Keating, 2009, pp. 38–50). I view this as a format or model for my own theorizing of self through my stories.

> ... conocimiento is reached via creative acts—writing, art-making, dancing, healing, teaching, mediation, and spiritual activism—both mental and somatic (the body, too, is a forma as well as site of creativity). (p. 542)

I expand on feminist writing practice by also including and performing my visual testimonio. Visual testimonios are a performative practice of nepantla, an act of living in-between worlds. Through visual testimonios, I theorize by performing images as text. Gloria Anzaldúa (Anzaldúa 1999; Anzaldúa& Keating 2009, 2015) emphasizes that our stories, testimonios, and autohistorias are performances, that is, a collaborative effort between the reader and writer and/or artist. Writing performatively is a feminist/artist/act, an embodiment of the self through visual text. Visual testimonios is a decolonizing act using visual language to share one's testimonio; the artist/writer engages in autohistoria-teoría, theorizing through lived experience. Through a collaging of image and text, the maker/performer navigates tense, ambiguous, and shifting borderlands spaces (Sotomayor & García, 2023).

Because theorizing and knowledge building has historically been in the hands of dominant Anglo culture, and POC have been excluded, it is critical that we (POC) create and hold theorizing spaces, as through "our own approaches and methodologies, we transform that theorizing space" (Anzaldúa, 1990, p. xxv). By theorizing (making sense) of our experiences, we are researching ourselves, our historical contexts, and critically reflecting on self and our social realities. Students and people of color need autohistoria-teoría as a vehicle and path to rewrite histories and cross borders with new knowledge and methods of theorizing. We need autohistoria-teoría to help us navigate in-between spaces, to critically look at situations and their contexts (what's behind them), and to form "our own categories and theoretical models for patterns we uncover" (Anzaldúa, 1990, p. xxv). We need autohistoria-teoría because it includes critical self-reflection, lived experiences, transformations, creative acts, historical contexts, feelings of not-belonging, intuition, re-imagining, myth/symbology, and spirituality as core characteristics in creating one's story.

The holistic experience through the path of conocimiento emerges "from opening all your senses, consciously inhabiting your body and decoding its symptoms..." (Anzaldúa & Keating, 2015, p. 120). The unquenchable thirst for knowing oneself and longing for our true selves to emerge from the depths of our being through intuitive and spiritual awakening is fundamental. Creative expression is an inherent characteristic of conocimiento: "through creative engagements, you embed your experiences in a larger frame of reference, connecting your personal struggles with those of other beings on the planet, with the struggles of the Earth itself" (Anzaldúa & Keating, 2015, p. 119). By holistic practice, Anzaldúa positions all aspects of one's life in relationship to each other and to other people.

My interpretation is that part of Anzaldúa's vision for peace and love for self and others comes through a pursuit of balance through spiritual practice. For Anzaldúa, "spirituality is a symbology system.... Through spirituality we seek balance and harmony with our environment" (Anzaldúa & Keating, 2015, pp. 38–39). Because of this desire to understand oneself, circumstances in our life will occur that unveil aspects of who we are and what we thought our realities were. The inside and outside, private and public realities and contradictions seek balance within ourselves. This is often a painful experience, but it is a catalyst for transformation through nepantla—growth through difficulty. Anzaldúa's unique inclusion of spirituality with theory is a crucial component. She writes: "Although contemporary theories of identity leave out our innermost spiritual core identity, I'm interested in the connective membrane between the interiority and the exteriority of subjectivity" (Anzaldúa & Keating, 2015, p. 36).

As I travel through my own autohistoria-teoría-izing, a path has been forged into existence through my own experiences and theorizing of them. I reflect on my own upbringing and identity markers.

Although my father, from an early age, racially labeled me white, and claimed my **Spanish** heritage, in doing so he denied:
my indigenous **Taíno** roots and my **Arab** ancestry.

I grew **up** with consistent feelings of not-belonging. *At home I was told I was a White American citizen—yet I did not feel like one in the schools and* *churches I participated in. Called racists slurs at school and not quite belonging in 'American' culture with my friends, I felt displaced.*

   _____My father drew a border for my   race
                  citizenship
                  historical contexts
<u>myths for me to embody</u>
As I began to belong to myself.............my identity <u>transformed</u>
I identify as Latina……….. as a person of color.
             fragments of my lived experiences, a
sense of not-belonging
      shared U.S. historical context
      my cultural roots

A Resilient People: Taínos

The Indigenous, Taino lineage that is barely recognized today as living, due to the Spanish genocide centuries ago in the Caribbean. The Taíno civilization indigenous to the Greater Antilles-Caribbean Sea (Hispaniola) flourished on the islands, including Cuba, Hispaniola (Haiti and the Dominican Republic), Jamaica, and Puerto Rico before and after the time when Christopher Columbus landed on the beaches of the New World in 1492. The Taíno people were targeted for genocide by the Spanish, and many were killed. Many historians date a mass genocide and death of the Taíno ancestry, culture, and beliefs at the hands of Columbus and the Spanish. However, in the last decade, historians have begun to revisit this theory and to realize that the Taíno people are not only alive and active in their dispersed communities, but are a relevant and strong presence in Indigenous culture and society in the Caribbean.[2] Taíno beliefs encompass the concept that all of life is cyclical and that we must go into ourselves to be able to go out into the world.

  The Banyan tree is also more commonly known in the Caribbean by its Taíno name, the ceiba tree. In Boríken,[3] the name that the Taínos originally gave Puerto Rico, the ceiba is the national tree, holding many symbolic meanings for the island with sacred Taíno beliefs. The Taíno indigenous people of Boríken believe that the ceiba tree is the balance of the world stretching its trunk through the underworld, the sea, through earth, up into the heavens.

The ceiba tree also references the Ba Coa, the wooden pole Taínos use to make holes in the ground to plant seeds for harvest. The ceiba tree is also a symbol for the Taíno's all-powerful cemi Ata Bey, Mother Earth, where all life begins, a symbol of resilience, hope, love, and a ladder between worlds, a portal to ascend to a higher spiritual dimension (Rouse, 1992). In 2017, Puerto Rico suffered a horrible hurricane, named Maria by meteorologists, that devastated much of the island, including Vieques,[4] part of Puerto Rico's 51-acre coastal park where endangered sea turtles and pelicans live and which was formerly a military base for the United States. On Vieques, there is a 400-year-old ceiba tree regarded as a sacred history of Taíno religion.

When hurricane Maria hit in 2017, the area where the ceiba tree stood was devastated, left leafless and damaged, with knobby broken limbs left lying around its thick trunk. However, in early 2019 the ceiba tree miraculously put forth its pink, lily-like blossoms, offering renewed hope to Boricuas (Puerto Ricans) on the island. Ceiba trees don't bloom consistently; they need the exact conditions after the tree absorbs and stores enough energy to produce bright, sugary blossoms. The La ceiba tree from Puerto Rico intensifies for me the initial metaphor of the Banyan tree. Because of the symbolism of strength, it represents a reverence toward Taíno beliefs that also emerges organically through the blooming of the cieba. I ascribe the ceiba tree's conditions and nutritional needs to bloom to the knowledge needed and lost in order to grow—the strength and nutrients necessary for absorption in order to be able to blossom despite having endured pain, devastation, violence, and trauma. According to Taíno belief, difficulties in life such as necessary pain, allowed by Guakar, teach us strength and wisdom. Guakar is a warrior, the Lord of teaching trials, the spirit of tough life experiences from which we learn and mature, leading to wisdom (Rouse, 1992).

When I began reading about the Taíno people, I was struck by the assertion of genocide when I had experienced throughout my life trails that led me to my Taíno lineage. It was this re-searching that compelled me to look deeper, to re-member more deeply and ask inquisitive questions of relatives as I began to piece together these fragments. The first painting (see Figure 1) is a representation of the violence unleashed on the Taíno culture, people, and way of living in Puerto Rico.

Figure 4.1. *Borikên* (2020), acrylic on canvas, 32" x 24"; artist Leslie C. Sotomayor II. Used with permission.

For as long as I can remember, I have drawn spirals. I became aware that the Taíno language uses the symbol of a spiral to represent energy and sweet waters. This spoke to me as I immediately reflected on my artmaking journey, where I connect so much with bodies of water as metaphors, physical worlds that I cross often to the Caribbean. My paintings often have hues of blue, drowning the viewer. I can't help but think that in my core there is a connection to water as energy and sweetness for me. It replenishes me and permeates all of my work. The spiral is a place where many perspectives are present, and depending on where I am in my life, that perspective will shift (see Figure 2). The spiral signifies that the process of transformation and healing is ongoing; it has no beginning or end. It isn't neat: there are gaps, places of dislocation. Like the waves of the sea, it may be a gentle shifting or a tumultuous one. I will be able to see other perspectives that I could not see before. Like a ripple effect spiral in the sea, the energy that is present affects the whole and layers, bumps, and expands into each other.

Gloria Anzaldúa (2009) defines border art as "art and la frontera intersect in a liminal space where border people, especially artists, live in a state

Figure 4.2. *The Spiral* (2022), acrylic on canvas, 9" x 7"; artist Leslie C. Sotomayor II. Used with permission.

of "nepantla" (Anzaldúa & Keating, 2009, p. 180). She situated nepantla as a "natural habitat of artists," especially for artists who are binational, partaking in cultures or traditions of two or more worlds (Anzaldúa, 2009, p. 181). In situating border artists in a natural habit within nepantla, I interpret Anzaldúa's concept to indicate a portability of home. She explains in Chapter Two of Borderlands (1999) that she has always been immersed in her cultural roots, and because of this she has always had a place to draw from for her identity. She states: "I am a turtle, wherever I go I carry 'home' on my back" (Anzaldúa, 1999, p. 43). I apply this notion of turtles carrying their homes on their back wherever they go to border artists, and I unpack it in the next section in relation to my re-searching, re-membering my Taíno lineage (see Figure 3).

Utuado is a prime location where Taíno culture thrived, having a strong footprint of cave drawings, cemis, and many more landscape and physical artifacts. When I began learning about Taíno culture, much of it resonated with me, including themes about Taíno spiritual beliefs, myths, and stories that I

Figure 4.3. *Carrying My Home* (2022), acrylic on canvas, 12" x 9"; artist Leslie C. Sotomayor II. Used with permission.

began to notice in my observations, reflections, and research. In my thought labyrinth, the only way to get out is the same way you came in, reminding me of the Taíno creation story. In one part of the story, Guaguiona (the true cacique), after wandering, meets a Boitio. Boitio is someone who is not mesmerized by the distractions of the world and sees beyond into the World of Mystery and all things hidden. They can walk among the world and with their ancestors simultaneously (Caney Indigenous Spiritual Circle, Retrieved 2023). The river is symbolic of the Energy of Kaguana, who is love, fertility, abundance, and thriving—the embodiment of Feminine Energy.

Guanara is the sacred cave of Mother Earth, Guabonito, who lives near a river. Guaguiona must travel to the sacred chamber, Guanara of Guabonito. Guaguiona is given by Guabonito, the Guanin,[5] who now journeys to the depths of the world of death in order to reclaim his identity. When Guabanito exchanges energies with the boitio in the depths of the world of death, they are able to be healed. Once healed, they are reborn and, while being birthed and leaving the underworld, are given a new name. As they ascend from the underworld, they have begun a profound spiritual process into an expansive consciousness, allowing them passage to the three realms: upper world, middle world, and underworld.

In the next section, I share my visual plática testimonio and paintings as theorizing in tandem with my ancestral imprint.

Re-Searching in My Studio

> "It is through the eyes of the multiple consciousnesses of ONE that the consciousness of ALL sees ALL!"
>
> *(Taíno proverb)*

One's coming into awakening of consciousness is an individual experience with ripple effects that may affect collective consciousness, as the Taíno proverbs above states. It is the awakening of multiple consciousnesses coming together that facilitates the visibility of all as bridges and connections. My crossing and inhabiting of nepantla is so frequent in connection to who I am as a nepantlera border artist that I cannot separate one from the other. A nepantlera is one who chooses to be a border crosser, a mediator, crossing back and forth (Anzaldúa & Keating, 2015). I am always a border artist. I need to make work because it is who I am. My identity as a nepantlera border artist is always present—hyphenated with all the fragments of my daily life. I am here and there at all times. I carry my home with me wherever I go, like a turtle. Autohistoria-teoría, the blending "their cultural and personal biographies with memoir, history, storytelling, myth, and other forms of theorizing" (Anzaldúa & Keating, 2009, p. 9), is a bridge that enables border artists to bring together fragments of themselves through nepantla, as "journeys as a nepantlera whose liminal existence requires continuous shuttling across many borders . . ." (Bhattacharya & Payne, 2016, p. 14).

In the same spirit in which Anzaldúa reclaims parts of her history, autohistoria, by digging through her ancestral roots, I too have been mining through history to unearth parts of my identity that were previously unknown to me. As I overturned stones in my research, some pieces rang familiar on my journey: the Taíno myths, proverbs, and songs that I have grown up listening to in my family, for example. Only in recent years have I heard my father on two, maybe three occasions admit that his mother *may* have been Taíno. Growing up, what was emphasized was my grandfather's white Spanish blood. As I examined family photos of my late abuela, I was convinced that she was or had a Taíno lineage, with her long, dark black hair, her small stature and bronze skin.

I have named my journey *Nicoari* (sounds like "Nee Koah Ree"), which in Taíno vocabulary means valiant, brave, and spirited.

Cafe con leche in my abuelas cocina
        Batê, batê, batê la leche
                Climb the rocks
Finding the waterfalls en la montanas . . . . . . ahi, ahi
        We dive down into the water holes, refrescar
Setup the fire, bring the calderos, vamos a cocinar
We eat together sunning on the rocks
        Stories from our lips, rizas de nuestros vientres
        carried up the mountain
        Winding their way into caves, caves that were once
        ours in secret.
Stiff jaw line, deep faith—survival of your hands

Figure 4.4. *Cemis* (2020), acrylic on canvas, 16" x 18"; artist Leslie C. Sotomayor II. Cemis is the Taíno word for spirit, and all of the spirit deities are housed in this term. Used with permission.

Ata Bey, the Taíno matriarch from whom all life proceeds, is whole, and so are her creations (see Figure 5). Taíno spirituality emphasizes life and experiences as interconnectedness to the past, present, and future, with a vision of becoming whole and balanced in who we already are—who we were created to be. The search of our Whole Essence is a striving that Elder Ni Bon Te Ban explains as "to take back the Power of Our Lives into our Yukayekes" (Caney Circle Tribe, Retrieved 2023). Ata Bey is the female creatress ancestral spirit of the Taíno people. The divine mother Ata Bey holds multiple representations of her characteristics. According to the Caney Indigenous Spiritual Circle (Retrieved 2023), Ata Bey is the embodiment of Guar Ban Sesh (Spirit of violent Mother Nature), Ata Bey/Atabeira (mother earth, birth, fertility), Caguana (Spirit of love and affection), Karaya (Moon Spirit, human connection to the divine), and her twin sons, Yoka Hu (the Lord of life force) and Guakar (The Lord of trials, experience, and wisdom).

Figure 4.5. *Atabey* (2020), acrylic on canvas, 24" x 20"; artist Leslie C. Sotomayor II. Used with permission.

> ATA BEY ATA BEY—*from your cave I was born*
> *Brought forth from the darkness, created, formed*
> *Ata bey, who whispers your name? Touching your roots to the underworld, absorbing the waters . . . . . all yours. Drink, drink me up. Drink la mar.*

Upon further investigation, I learned that my abuela was from Utuado, Puerto Rico, mountainous countryside of the island rich in Taíno indigenous artifacts, beliefs, traditions, and spirituality. My abuela was said to be married at age 13 when my grandfather, a Puerto Rican with Spanish blood 14 years her senior, met her on her family's land in Utuado, Puerto Rico. He *took her as his wife*. They subsequently lived in Adjuntas, a neighboring town, and she would give birth to fourteen children, the first one dying at a few weeks old.

The Gua symbol in Taíno culture represents the male and female elements of nature (see Figure 6). Ata Bey gave birth to a male spirit, Yoca Hu (see Figure 7) and became a cosmic union, the cosmic mother, Ata Bey bore all of creation (Caney Circle, Retrieved 2023).

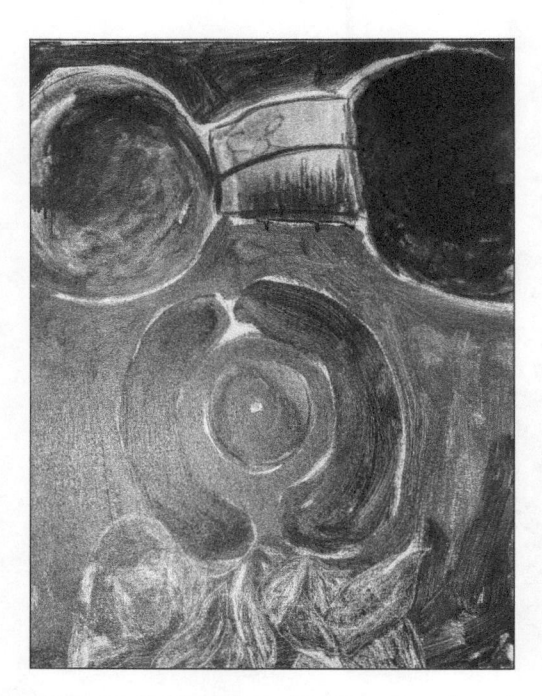

Figure 4.6. *El Sol y La Luna* (2020), acrylic and pastel on canvas, 16" x 18"; artist Leslie C. Sotomayor II. Used with permission.

Figure 4.7. *Yoca Hu* (2022), acrylic on canvas, 12" x 16"; artist Leslie C. Sotomayor II. Used with permission.

Curandera

    rock, stones, pebbles……...trails— machete in hand, cutting away at all that is….
                                  Obstruction: layers of hidden knowledge:
burned: drowned: torn: thrown: whispers::::

                                                 may have been Taína.
white Spanish sangre, studded with betrayal: desprecío.

    Buscando, buscando—looking for my dis-membered parts:

                looking for *her*
                her dark long black hair
                her small stature
                her bronze skin
                              I *re*-member
                                  guanimes
                                      myths, proverbs, songs

the ceiba tree in Borínken,
the land of the courageous ^(may we be courageous)
                                                                          the ceiba
S   t   r   e   t   c   h   i   n   g

Underworld
La mar
Earth
Heavens

                                          Ba Coa: harvest.

Ata Bey,
Mother Earth spirit,
          : resilience, hope, love, ladder, between

                                    "Tu eres"? Que es eso? Boricua,

Ata Bey : Guar Ban Sesh : Ata Bey/Atabeira : Caguana : Karaya : Yoka Hu : Guakar : Ata Bey: Ata Bey.

I wandered into the labyrinth : : the belly of the snake. Skin lost, expelled:::

Snake, shed skin:::: teeth
                    Incense burns at my altar: burns, burn, burning

Reflection

From Anzaldúa's theories of autohistoria-teoría, conocimiento, nepantla, and nepantlera, I offer a theoretical frame for bridging transnational spaces that embody an in-between space where the works of border artists, educators, and curators inhabit a temporal home. The temporal home fluctuates; it may be the classroom space, the artwork itself, or a curated gallery. As the "creative acts" occur, bridging is possible between people and experiences, allowing for "healing through our wounds" (Anzaldúa, 2009, 247). As we heal, we are able to take the fragments of our lived experiences and creative acts and re-construct ourselves and our identities. In my understanding, autohistoria-teoría and conocimiento are not dependent upon each other. However, in my experience, as I connect further into what the transformational recursive stages of conocimiento mean in my life, the deeper I am able to theorize about my personal experience through visual testimonios, writing, and studio practice. I have grappled in this chapter as a nepantlera, a border crosser within my own life and expanse of what scholarship is and, I imagine, can mean for myself. The combination of visual testimonio on the page and artwork interwoven with theory is a tapestry that engages the process of healing through my wounds as an embodied act, a form of spiritual activism.

Notes

1. There are seven stages that Gloria Anzaldúa explains in her conocimiento theory (Anzaldúa 2015: Sotomayor, 2022).
2. https://tainomuseum.org/?q=/taino/history/
3. Borikén: the Taíno indigenous name of the U.S. colonized territorial island of Puerto Rico.
4. Isla de Vieques is an island of Puerto Rico, and its name is Taíno for small island. Today the island is a national wildlife refuge, but until 2003 it was internationally known as a site for protests against the United States Navy's use of the island as a bombing range and testing ground..
5. Guanin: symbolic of the bright and shining sun and symbol of Cacique.

References

Anzaldúa, G. (1990). *Making face, making soul: Haciendo caras: Creative and critical perspectives by feminists of color* (1st ed.). Aunt Lute Books.
Anzaldúa, G. (1999). *Borderlands: La frontera: The new mestiza* (2nd ed.). Aunt Lute Books.
Anzaldúa, G., & Keating, A. (2009). *The Gloria Anzaldúa reader.* Duke University Press.
Anzaldúa, G.(2015). *A Light in the dark: Luz en lo oscuro: Rewriting identity, spirituality, reality.* Duke University Press.
Bhattacharya, K., & Payne, R. (2016). Mixing mediums, mixing selves: Arts-based contemplative approaches to border crossings. *International Journal of Qualitative Studies in Education, 29*(9), 1100–1117.
Caney Indigenous Spiritual Circle, Retrieved 2023. https://caneycircle.wordpress.com/gua/
Sotomayor, L. (2022). *Teaching in/between: Curating educational spaces with autohistoria-teoría and conocimiento.* Vernon Press.
Sotomayor, L. & García, C. (2023). 'Nepantlando: A Borderlands Approach to Curating, Art Practice, and Teaching' in Sharma, M., & Alexander, A. (Eds.). (2023).The Routledge

Companion to Decolonizing Art, Craft, and Visual Culture Education. Taylor & Francis. Chicago.

Rouse, I. (1992). *The Taínos: Rise and decline of the people who greeted Columbus*. Yale University Press.

Sague-Machiran, M. (2016). *Canoa: Taíno Indigenous Dream River Journey*. Iuniverse.

Strayhorn, T. L. (2012). *College students' sense of belonging: A key to educational success for all students*. Routledge.

FIVE

Do No Harm: An Autoethnography of a Novice Research Supervisor Learning to Dwell Within and Stand Apart

Joanne Yoo

When helping hurts

After COVID-19 hit, there were waves of losses in our faculty. International students left in droves, courses were discontinued, and there was an onslaught of redundancies. With only a handful of staff left, I found myself inheriting a Ph.D. student who was in the final stages of his candidacy. His previous two supervisors had both left the university, and I was quickly brought on board. My inexperience was brushed over, and I was left to make sense of loose ends. *How hard could it be?* All I had to do was to read, listen, and nudge him in the desired direction. I held onto this belief until it was time to provide feedback, when I suddenly found myself at a loss. Long drafts of chapters were sent through over the weekend, and I pushed through the fatigue to make sense of complex concepts that I had a passing knowledge of. *Where do I go from here? What steps do I take?* I felt pressured to be a "good" supervisor who provided useful feedback, but instead, I felt like a raging bull that left a trail of destruction. I marked up page after page, unable to maneuver around the delicately interwoven strands of thought and feeling. Disturbed by the possibility that my attempts to "help" were actually doing harm, I became too afraid to say anything.

The responsibility of his candidacy weighed heavily on my inexperienced shoulders, and I felt as if I were walking along a fraying tightrope. Ellis (2000) touches on these difficulties of providing supportive feedback in her role as a reviewer. She navigates this "hardest part" by interrogating whether her response is constructive or not (p. 276). She rewrites sections in a more "encouraging manner" to ensure that she does not cause any unnecessary harm. Not wanting to invalidate another's story, she writes, "I ask if there is a better way to say something critical yet protect the author's sense of self. I remind myself that not only is the writer's scholarship on the line, but perhaps their personal identity as well" (p. 276). Mindful of how feedback can impact the vulnerabilities of both beginner and more seasoned writers, she works hard to ensure that it is both "critical and supportive" (p. 276). Ellis (2000) continues to check on her own frames of reference, asking herself, "Is this a topic I know little about? I have built in biases about? I have not experienced? I have experienced differently?" (p. 274). Not only does she question the validity of the writer's perspectives; she also reflects on her capacity to construct an informed response.

Inclusive conversations about 'quality'

We need to be reflexive about our conceptual frameworks because they are shaped by our unique experiences. If they are not inclusive of other ways of knowing, our accounts are limited and superficial at best. Academic disciplines also have their own particular conventions and ways of framing knowledge. For example, when we write for an academic audience, we conform to each journal's stylistic preferences, but when writing for the general public, we may find that our readers value the traits of a good story, such as "fidelity, coherence, generosity, wisdom, imagination, honesty, respect and verisimilitude" (Van Maanen, 1988, p. 33). There are also different degrees of creativity, depending on one's methodology. Academics who gravitate toward more creative and narrative forms of writing may have more expansive measures for assessing value. They may look for nuanced details that reveal the complexities of the everyday, or non-linear plot lines that depict the subjective experience of time, as well as the author's capacity to critique their world views and to demonstrate ethical awareness (Bochner, 2000). Their understanding of impact may differ entirely, as rather than measuring the citation index of their publications, they may desire an engaging story that evokes a conversation and moves our hearts (Bochner, 2000).

By the nature of their work, reviewers undertake this critical process, sifting through the multitude of papers that compete for limited publication space. Reviewers and editors ensure that papers with the best *fit* get published, but the review process can be arduous. Ellis (2000) provides an insider perspective by detailing the steps taken when reviewing academic papers. She demonstrates how the act of reading itself discloses, stating, "If I read the whole paper without stopping to evaluate cognitively from a distance—well that tells me something. The work has engaged me. If I read the whole story, stopping frequently to think about details of my experience, my memories or feelings called forth by the piece, then the work has evoked me" (p. 274). I nod my head as I take in these words. If I read a text without stopping to puzzle something out logically, then I know that I have been engrossed in it, similar to how I feel when reading a good piece of fiction. But if something resonates so strongly that it stirs up a memory, connecting me to something that I may have personally lived, then my level of engagement multiplies. I have interacted with the text, making it my own by weaving in my experiences and worldview. Such writing is inclusive, since it can encompass the voices of others. The narration of the story becomes a shared act in which voices mingle together to create new knowledge. The way I slow down to linger within and to engage Ellis's words provides evidence of this fact.

When her logical mind is aroused, Ellis (2000) stands at a distance to consider the story as an observer. Such distancing allows her to move to and fro in a critical discussion with the author's words. More often than not, however, Ellis (2000) finds herself ". . . questioning the logic of the story, what's left out, underdeveloped, unconvincing, disorganized. What's too chaotic, or not chaotic enough. [Since] the piece literally interrupts itself . . . it may mean the story has no narrative soul. It has not engaged, evoked, or provoked me sufficiently. I remain disconnected, outside the experience" (p. 274). Her reading continues to be interrupted because of the paper's lack of coherence and fluidity. She is left unsatisfied with how the story is told and developed. To clarify why she feels this way, she engages in a closer second reading, carefully annotating the margins to link her initial impressions with the actual text itself. When gut feelings align with evidence, Ellis (2000) finds it easier to reach a decision about a paper, but when they don't, she resumes her reading, acting as an "editor . . . to make a determination among [her] own internally conflicting views" (p. 274). Carefully, line by line, she reads. Such a close and thoughtful reading is vital because "Only rarely is a manuscript all good or all bad" (p. 274). A good reviewer can recognize these glimmers of potential and can bring them to the surface. By reflecting these glimpses back to the writer, they can spur the writer onto a path of growth.

Harm

Harm appears in many forms. A writer is made vulnerable as they put their work "out there" under the scrutiny of anonymous others, exposed to their criticism, praise, and suggestions for improvement. All researchers have experienced the academic community's double-edged sword as they publish their work. This vulnerability is voiced by Rawlins (Chawla & Rawlins, 2004) as he reflects on his work as a Ph.D. supervisor:

> I believe we are all so vulnerable and in need of confirmation in the academy that we tend to forget just how truly vulnerable our students (as well as our colleagues) are. I believe that in our hearts and minds, we all need for others to read our words and speak with us thoughtfully. (p. 969)

The value of care and kindness within the supervisory relationship had stood out because I was such an unremarkable doctoral student. My lack of direction was evident within the transient life I had been living, floating around overseas teaching English, bored with my job, and unsure of the future. When I heard that a close friend had started a Ph.D., I thought, *Why not me?* I soon found myself enrolled in a doctoral program while continuing to work abroad. Without clear guiding questions and too busy enjoying weekends hanging out with friends, I was desperately falling behind. My principal supervisor eventually admonished me after I failed to submit work yet again, and rather than buckling down and getting things done, I continued to dig myself into an even greater hole. My secondary supervisor, who was unburdened by the deadlines, took on a different approach. She engaged with whatever I sent her in a conversation, regardless of how limited it was, sharing what she was thinking and feeling as she read my work. *Yes, I feel this too. I was also wondering about.... You know what I like about this....* All of her comments formed a lifeline that kept me on the grueling path to completion.

Reflecting on my own experiences of being "supervised," I sought to emulate my secondary supervisor. She didn't really act like a supervisor in the formal sense by attempting to "oversee" my work (Dictionary.com, n.d-a). She was more like a knowledgeable and trustworthy friend who kept me company through the rocky and uneven bits of path (Dictionary.com, n.d-b). Feedback, when it was given, not only left my self-esteem intact, but it made me excited about exploring my ideas. *I liked how you wrote . . . isn't it interesting how X says*. . . . I was not just a tardy student, but I was also someone who showed promise. *Maybe I do have something worthwhile to share here*. She saw potential and could reflect it back to me through the genuine interest she showed in my ideas, and this reignited my own curiosity. *So close. I was so close to giving up so often*. These memories bring me back to my own Ph.D. student, who had to juggle work and study during a pandemic while accommodating the demands of a new supervisor. Without someone encouraging him to trust in himself and to speak up, he would have found it hard to express his unique voice.

Holding up a mirror

To be truly *seen*. It is a remarkable occurrence. We can live with someone for decades and not feel this way. Alternatively, we can meet someone for a few short moments and feel like we have known them our whole lives. This feeling of being understood is even more tenuous because of how little we disclose. Given how busy we are, it is rare to find someone who can take the time to get to know us beyond the social masks we wear. The actions of *seeing* and being *seen*, however, form the basis of a meaningful supervisory relationship. Chawla reflects on the mutual reflexivity enabled by a supportive mentoring relationship with Rawlins, her Ph.D. supervisor (Chawla & Rawlins, 2004). She depicts a turning point in their relationship, where she shares a significant but non-academic piece of writing titled *Two Journeys* to provide an intimate glimpse into her world. She invites him into this vulnerable space because she yearns to be understood. *Will he accept the person that I am?* she ponders. Will he "get" me? By going through this story "line by line," she dives deep into the essence of her story, and in turn, Rawlins feels honored by her trust (Chawla & Rawlins, 2004, p. 968). She gives him a little slice of her vulnerability so that he can see her in the way she recognizes herself.

This feeling of being *seen* and *known* is the starting point of Chawla's self-awareness as an academic writer, as she writes, "For the first time in my life, someone began to explain to me that I did have my own style of writing, which was an embodied narrative stance. I knew that I was an above-average writer, but I never knew why and how" (Chawla & Rawlins, 2004, p. 969). The supervisory relationship holds up a mirror that reflects her rich, embodied presence back to herself. Rawlins brings to her attention the vibrant voice that makes her so skillful at her craft. He reiterates this point by defining reflexivity in terms of a conversation, where we get a sense of how we exist through how we relate to others, asserting that "Enabling reflexivity is neither preoccupied with self nor an imposition on others. It is the kind of reflexivity that enables and empowers; and as such, performing such reflexivity enables analogous reflexivity in others" (Chawla & Rawlins, 2004, p. 972). Thus a relational state of being constitutes an ethical form of awareness because it embodies care and reciprocity (Tracy, 2010). We develop this reciprocal relationship of trust and respect as we care for others by being attentive to their stories. To perceive the supervisory process as a mutually reciprocal relationship of care is to focus on the individual and to ". . . maximis[e] of all that is subjective, inward, personal; here a relationship is lived, not examined, and a person, not an object, emerges; a person who feels, chooses, believes, acts, not as an automaton, but as a person" (Rogers, 1961, p. 277). Maximizing the subjective means to value the person rather than simply their work; it is to commune with and to relate to, rather than trying to manipulate, fix, or control.

Within a supportive relationship, we can learn to see ourselves clearly. Rawlins's feedback on Chawla's writing acts as this clear mirror that reflects her rich capacity to ". . . see and write [her] own evolving worlds with a literary eye, with the open and expanding soul of the artist who has her own and others' humanity in mind" (Chawla & Rawlins, 2004, p. 972). A similar situation emerged with my secondary supervisor through an email exchange about a book I had written almost 15 years after I completed my doctorate. Knowing what a poor student I had been, I still felt a lingering shame and regret as I recalled this time. It was therefore very surprising to read her humbling words of praise:

> Thank you, Joanne. That is so kind of you. Likewise, you made a great impression on me, including as a PhD student. Your thesis was wonderful and it is just lovely for me to see your career thriving—and this book will be such a valuable contribution to the field. We need more voices in the qualitative space. You write so beautifully and eloquently, so whatever you write will be filled with your distinctive voice of empathy, sensitivity and insight. (J. Manuel, personal communication, March 30, 2021)

My candidacy was a dark and directionless period. Although I had managed to catch up in the final months, I was not proud of the work I had submitted. *She would not remember me. I was a terrible student.* But this email had negated my gloomy version of the story, providing me with a different perspective. My brain stirred into action, attempting to formulate a new story as I read her words . . . *beautifully and eloquently . . . voice of empathy, sensitivity and insight.* These words echoed loud and clear as I contemplated them, revealing an image of self that I had not considered before. *Perhaps the false steps were just a part of the learning process.* Her words formed the missing pieces of the puzzle, giving me insight into how my struggles as a doctoral student may have shaped the writer who I was now.

To *see* is to dwell within

Empathy or the imaginative capacity to *dwell within* is instrumental to deep understanding. Emotional awareness enables us to consider the perspectives of others so that we can access spaces that are not originally our own. Empathy is accordingly essential for qualitative researchers as they seek to better understand human experience. Ellingson (1998) provides an example of *dwelling within* through her ethnographic research of cancer sufferers. She intimately understands their suffering since she had also experienced the debilitating impact of cancer first-hand, so much so that at one point, her "distant and impersonal sympathy" transforms into a full-blown, embodied flashback of her own treatment, in which she was gagging so heavily she could not even breathe (p. 492). Her reflexivity allows her to appreciate the value of embodied knowing in inquiry, as she writes:

> Any researcher could prepare him or herself by doing library research on effects of and treatments for cancer. However, having the knowledge embedded in my mind is different. . . . This bodily knowing and remembering is rooted in the physical experience of treatment, rather than in mental grasping of abstract terms and concepts. A second function of my cancer experiences is that they increase my capacity for and willingness to empathize and sympathize with patients. (Elllingson, 1998, p. 495)

Making sense through the filter of one's personal experiences can enrich. Ellingson's (1998) account on the trials of cancer treatment embodies authority, as she describes cancer through how it ravaged her body. The vividness of her account gives it credibility. Descriptions of her field work are punctuated by flashbacks of her cancer treatment. Her description of a patient's bland referral to an endoscopy triggers a memory of a technician's insistent urge to "Swallow it. Swallow it" (p. 493). She finds herself back there, trying to swallow an overly large rubber tube that is shoved roughly into the back of her mouth until she is gagging and suffocating. The full misery of that moment is captured in her helplessness and the technician's lack of empathy. The intimacy of her lived experience injects life into words. An endoscopy is no longer just a medical term but becomes a full bodily experience that reminds us of our mortality. Such reminders bring us back to our common human condition, which inspires resonance.

Resonance can be so powerful that it holds sway over our logical minds. I experienced its impact through a paper I had written outside my discipline, which should have been rejected since it did not conform to the other publications in the journal. It was accepted because it had caught someone's notice. The paper was about writing creatively to explore retirement, and although gerontology was not my area of expertise, the methodology of writing as inquiry provided an entry point. I wrote to inquire into my own fledgling thoughts about retirement and how it could shape my academic career by diverting me from a mindless pursuit of success. The reverberation felt by the journal's editor was fortunately strong enough to momentarily silence her logical mind. She acknowledged her hesitation in sending it out for review, explaining, "The piece resonated strongly with me when I first read it, so was willing to send this out for review despite it being outside the norm for this journal" (n.a, personal communication, January 13, 2020). A similar feeling of resonance was experienced by a reviewer, who gave the manuscript a second reading because it gave her pause for thought, as she disclosed:

> I couldn't help but think to myself as I read that we as gerontologists talk about how we don't really include the experiences of actual ageing people. The tie in here between auto-ethnographic writing and writing as generative are really compelling. I found myself relating a lot of what is written here to my own experiences. In short, I do think the author has provided a compelling revision that would be a really interesting contribution. (n.a, personal communication, January 13, 2020)

The paper equally resonated for a reader, who composed a poem in response. He expressed a desire to try autoethnographic writing to explore his own lived experiences of retirement. In his email, he wrote:

> In this article you have included many inspiring ideas for coping with the tundra of retirement (in my case after 58 years in my profession), and I was struck by the phrases, sentences, and linguistic elegance you quoted and created in it. Some of the phrases and sentences in my attempt at an autoethnographic poem are extracted directly from the article; others have been edited, twisted, or embellished from my own limited quiver of linguistic arrows. I appreciate greatly the ideas, attitudes, and insights in this article. (L.L. Lapointe, personal communication, March 17, 2020)

Resonance creates a means of dwelling within. In the case of reading academic work, resonance can initiate a conversation. We flitter in and out of the writer's world and our own, moving fluently between both because they are on a similar wavelength. This alignment of wavelengths brings to the surface what has yet to be understood, so that it can be appreciated and known. *Yes, this makes sense. I have also felt this when. . . .* From this point of familiarity, thoughts can branch out into multiple directions as lines of possibility take flight. *In my life this looks like . . . so this is what was happening when. . . .* The stronger the resonance, the deeper and more genuine our relationship becomes. The writer's words appear trustworthy since we can verify them with our own experiences, and this leads to a feeling of oneness. *I feel a sense of solidarity. . . .* We feel known and valued within this relationship since we see ourselves reflected back to us, in all its richness. . . . *I can see myself in you. . . .* These tacit exchanges underpin the immersive reading process, where we engage with what we read to better understand our lives.

To see is to stand apart

The movement between *dwelling within* and *standing apart* underpins the inquiry process. Through dwelling empathetically within the words we read, we can deeply experience the encounters disclosed. Moreover, by standing apart, we can gain perspective by seeing things through a broader lens. In terms of academic inquiry, standing apart helps us to move away from the subjective lens to engage in a wider scholarly discussion. Bondi (2013) provides an analogy within a psychotherapeutic encounter, describing how understanding lies in the ability to ". . . at least temporarily, to disentangle and accurately distinguish one's own mental state from that of the other . . ." (p. 13). She refers to this external perspective as the "third position" (p. 13). Standing back creates a distance so that we can see beyond our emotional filter, as she states: "Moving into this third position is therefore exactly what we do as researchers, when we explore, and write about the living of lives, whether our own or others" (p. 13). This reflexive space helps us to gain perspective and to process our encounters. In the context of receiving feedback, we stand back so that we can move beyond our knee-jerk reactions, as Bondi (2013) comments:

> I doubt that I am alone in often finding it difficult—at least initially—to receive feedback on my manuscripts, especially when that feedback comes in the disembodied form of anonymous reviews. I can find myself unable to take in the written words and I can experience even the slightest hint of criticism as an outrageous attack. Sometimes my faith in my own work collapses at this moment and I join with the imagined attack regarding my efforts as useless and unworthy. While I usually get over and move beyond this kind of initial response (thank goodness), when immersed in this experience it is as if I have become inseparable from my own manuscript rather than it remaining separate from me.

When we are so invested in our work, it is difficult to separate ourselves from the "one-ness with the world and with ourselves," but by taking a step back, we can perceive our encounters with greater clarity (Bondi, 2013, p. 14). Distance allows us to generate a symbolic representation of our encounters so that we can witness them. For example, through writing this paper, I could distance myself from the image of a rampaging bull to revisit my dilemmas through the lens of my secondary supervisor and the stories of other academics. I could take on board their perspectives to discover the paradoxical flow of dwelling within and standing apart underpinning the feedback process. Bondi (2013) asserts that the opposite of such meaning-making manifests in trauma, which is a state of not being able to move on. She relates how this reflexive gap often disappears with trauma, as it is an "experience that persists in unaltered, unprocessed form," where we continue to relive or alienate ourselves from our encounters (p. 15). We fail to move on since we are stuck in Groundhog Day, constantly replaying our trauma or denying that it ever occurred. Through generating a symbolic representation, however, we can take on an alternate position to shift our perspective. And by forming a different interpretation of an encounter, we can find a different path forward. In the context of receiving negative feedback, we may eventually move away from an overly defensive stance to see things from the reviewer's perspective.

The same holds true when providing feedback. By standing back and separating oneself from one's feedback, we can see it through the lens of the receiver. Although it wasn't easy to place myself in such a position, I would find myself there when my Ph.D. student would query my feedback. When our opinions differed, I tried to stand apart to see things from his perspective by asking myself, *What did I mean by this comment? How else could he have written it?* These questions would identify certain gaps, such as *What about your story? How do your experiences shape . . . ?* They reflected my desire to better understand the personal stories and intent driving his inquiry. Moments of not seeing eye to eye sparked the reflective process, highlighting the intricate movement between *dwelling within* and *standing apart* underpinning the knowing act. Standing back, without the capacity to dwell within, prevented me from perceiving the world as he saw it. Dwelling within, without the capacity to stand back, disconnected my student and I from larger frameworks structuring his discussion. Standing back, and asking him about his lived experiences, also created a reflective gap where he could hear his personal stories reflected back to him. This helped him to trust in the authority of his words, as he could see how they connected to ongoing discussions. He could move from the intimacy of a lived encounter to comprehend broader arguments, affirming how ". . . life as subjectively experienced is the key to understanding the cultural and the sociological" (Richardson, 1995, p. 195). Through this intricate process between dwelling within and standing back, we could actively shape the meaning-making process.

The lightest of touches

Although I am not a medical doctor, I still hold fast to the oath of *doing no harm*, realizing that behind every manuscript is a person, just like me, who is struggling to *make sense* of their circumstances. I do not wield a scalpel but acknowledge that any response I make regarding another person's work can be equally cutting. Richardson's (1995) words embody this pain of having her work criticized, relaying, "Her assault on the poem felt more humiliating than any public criticism I have had of my sociological work" (p. 198). The pain of this memory makes her avoid individually critiquing ethnographic papers, as she writes, "How rude it would be to praise someone's work, perhaps, and not another's. How painful are invidious comparisons, much less outright criticism.... If I could not say something equally "nice" about all of them, I would rather say nothing at all about any of them" (Richardson, 1995, p. 197). Mindful of the pain she may inadvertently cause, she treads softly. I desire such nimble feet, sensing that my feedback as a research supervisor can potentially do more harm than good. Like Rogers (1961), I recognize the challenges of providing meaningful feedback, and affirm how "... anything that can be taught to another is relatively inconsequential and has little or no significant influence on behaviour" (p. 276). Rogers (1961) accordingly advises us to focus on our own learning rather than to teach another, because "real" learning is "self-discovered, self-appropriated... personally appropriated and assimilated in experience" (p. 277). Approaching my supervisory work as a *learner* is to continue honing the craft of feedback with empathetic finesse, leaving barely a mark as I attempt to restore curiosity, joy, and a lightness of spirit through maintaining a delicate balance between *dwelling within* and *standing apart*. Indeed, when my supervisory relationship seemed to be going well, I felt myself moving fluently between these opposing poles.

Seeing and being *seen* involves the lightest of touches. With each touch, I try to make sense as accurately as possible, trusting that whatever words I share will be most "generally and genuinely satisfying" (Rogers, 1961, p. 277). A light touch also encompasses a trust in one's own sense-making and a knowledge that our feet are agile enough to quickly shift direction if needed. We intuit these steps that carry us into half-lit spaces, accommodating any wrong turns we make along the way, or as Rogers (1961) remarks, "Letting my experience carry me on, in a direction which appears to be forward, onward goals that I can but dimly define, as I try to understand at least the current meaning of that experience" (p. 277). Stepping lightly in the flow of our experiences, toward goals that we barely make out, we continue to remain open to new ways of inquiry so that we can press on when one road is blocked, rather than simply stumbling around in the dark.

References

Bochner, A. (2000). Criteria against ourselves. *Qualitative Inquiry, 6*(2), 266–272.

Bondi, L. (2013). Research and therapy: Generating meaning and feeling gaps. *Qualitative Inquiry, 19*(1), 9–19.

Chawla, D., & Rawlins, W. K. (2004). Enabling reflexivity in a mentoring relationship. *Qualitative Inquiry, 10*(6), 963–978.

Dictionary.com. (n.d.-a). Supervise [Def. 1]. In Dictionary.com. Retrieved December 9, 2022, from https://www.dictionary.com/browse/supervise

Dictionary.com. (n.d.-b). Guide [Def. 1, 2]. In Dictionary.com. Retrieved December 9, 2022, from https://www.dictionary.com/browse/supervise

Ellingson, L. (1998). "Then you know how I feel": Empathy, identification, and reflexivity in fieldwork. *Qualitative Inquiry, 4*(4), 492–514.

Ellis, C. (2000). Creating criteria: An ethnographic short story. *Qualitative Inquiry, 6*(2), 273–277.

Richardson, L. (1995). Writing-stories: Co-authoring "The sea monster," a writing-story. *Qualitative Inquiry, 1*(2), 189–203.

Rogers. (1961). *On becoming a person: A therapist's view of psychotherapy*. Houghton Mifflin.

Tracy, S. J. (2010). Qualitative quality: Eight "big-tent" criteria for excellent qualitative research. *Qualitative Inquiry, 16*(10), 837–851.

Van Maanen, J. (1988). *Tales of the field*. University of Chicago Press.

SIX

Unmaking Frames through Poetic Photographic Inquiry: When Silence Meets Arts Meets Method Meets Resistance

Reyila Hadeer

THE COLLEGE OF EDUCATION WHERE I am completing my doctoral studies is located at the center of the Michigan State University campus, next to the Red Cedar River that flows across the Lansing-East Lansing area of Michigan. I remember in my geography textbook in middle school in Northwest China, we learned the state of Michigan is a state in the Great Lakes region of the upper Midwestern United States (US). We were also being tested about the names of the five Great Lakes in North America, and we also memorized that the United States is a global power and the most developed country in the world.

As I started my graduate studies here in the College of Education, I often observed the building from the outside with awe, curiosity, and a bit of nervousness. The building is red, and the big glass walls reflect the dazzling sunshine, igniting some kind of unsettling fire inside me. As a so-called international student from the so-called "East," growing up in a small town in Northwest China, I was often afraid I did not fit into this architecture that looks serious, solid, and unshakable at the center of a U.S. university. Every day, I walked by the Red Cedar River next to it. The river is flowing with the shape of a landscape. Sometimes fast, sometimes slow, sometimes it looks static. Occasionally, there are also times when the water does not respect the human-made landscapes. When there is flooding, the water unapologetically expands across all the boundaries that are designed to regulate it and shows its disobedience to the unreasonable design.

Uyghurs like me are considered to have originated from the Turkic ethnicity who primarily live in Northwest China. Significant diasporic communities of Uyghurs exist in the Central Asian countries, Europe, Northern America, and other places around the world. In my transnational journey, I have witnessed how the voices of Uyghur people are constantly drowned out by Chinese national discourse and Western academic essentialist stances. Currently, most studies embrace the positivist paradigm when they discuss Uyghurs and their representation. Researchers with a Chinese background tend to portray the minority as a passive subject that receives the help from dominant ethnic groups within the Chinese nation-state (see, e.g., Teng & Ma, 2005; Zhao, 2011; Zhou, 2001). Similarly, researchers with a Western background tend to look at Uyghur people as oppressed groups without acknowledging their agency (see, e.g., Bovingdon, 2004; Dwyer, 2005; Shichor, 2005). To some degree, one could argue that most studies about the Uyghur largely appear to be conducted *on* as opposed to *with* or *by* Uyghur researchers (Crowley, Hadeer, & Yu, 2021).

In my transnational lived experiences as an Uyghur woman, my body has been laid down and served as a battlefield of beliefs, others and mine. Discourses have been imposed on me, and different parts of them have become more dominant based on where I am in a larger social-global context at a particular moment. Sometimes, one wins over the other, scaring the others away. The hierarchy among discourses on gender, identity, religion, sexuality, race, and so on changes with time and place. I am the only one who seems to never win. Yet, I carry these discourses in order to just survive in a complex world. But it does not matter for those discourses. These discourses are ideologies with agendas. Moving within the cracks, "I" have always been yearning for something that can go beyond ideologies. Something in another dimension.

After entering the Western academia, while I am privileged to gain access to tremendous resources to explore knowledge, I sense the pressure of outside discourses stronger than ever before. Since I began my doctoral program, much of the time, people around me in academic settings ask me to engage in conversation. They tell me academia, literature reviews, and academic writing is a conversation. They keep asking who the people I want to have a conversation with are, what my field is, where I belong, and what I am against. I'm rushed into making decisions when I don't even know what the conversation is about, what they are talking about, or how I should engage. Why are they rushing me to take a stance and speak? I feel anxious. What does that mean to refuse to have these conversations? I choose silence.

At a moment during my doctoral study journey, the College of Education, an institution of impressive stature, epistemically and materially, suddenly

Figure 6.1. Photography, R. Hadeer (2020).

became small for me. Sometimes when I express myself, I start to feel like people around me are arguing with me. Sometimes sitting in a doctoral seminar, I could not distinguish complaints and critiques. Sometimes I have found myself looking for answers to what my genuine curiosity provokes in me in other buildings on campus.

When I am carrying my camera and tripod for my photography class, learning how to frame what I see in a 35 millimeter rectangle frame, my spirit of inquiry is set alight. It reminds me of my cousin in my childhood who has taught me how to pitch a hole on a grape leaf, and observe the world from a different perspective. Through the grape leaves, my cousin and I often tried to put the poplar tree in front of us and the mountains in the far distance in the same frame, wondering if we could find familiar poplar trees behind those mountains surrounding our home.

Other times in my doctoral study journey, I'm moving my body silently in a yoga studio, figuring out how to use as little muscular energy as possible so that the subtler wave-like motion of breath can flow through the form. As I move my body quietly up and down, it reminds me of how my grandma gently moves her body in a similar way on a rectangular Muslim prayer mat, "jinimaz," five times a day. It is her everyday routine to pray and connect with her Allah in a moment of silence.

I have wondered why I had to go outside my own building to look for answers to questions related to the nature of transnational education in the ways I wanted to approach it. Why was this the case? It was not that there wasn't enough to be known inside the walls of my own institutional building or the discourse inside the field. However, the ways of knowing and critiquing the world had become too contrived by the insistence on foundational knowledge, the peer-pressure of dead people, and institutional readings became detached from my familiar senses developed in my own lived experiences. I always found that I was yearning for more. As I allow myself to wonder and play freely by crossing boundaries and disciplines, it gradually becomes more and more clear for me that: what I am looking for is the kind of knowledge that enriches my experience, transcendental to matter, to the material.

Figure 6.2. Photography, R. Hadeer (2020).

Shifting the frame

"Why do your photographs always have a radical eye searching for what is beyond?" One of my professors made a comment on a small informal photography project I created. This simple comment inspired me, made me pause and re-visit the photographs I took in my everyday life. Why have I never thought about analyzing the photos I took by myself? Why did I take those photos in the first place? What does it say about me? One simple, inspiring comment of my mentor encouraged me to de-familiarize myself with the photos I take, and reconnect with them again with a researcher's eye. I started to search for a theme in those photographs that I have created for myself in my smartphone. I notice I have always been drawn to the wildflowers escaping from the fence, weeds growing in the cracks on the sidewalk, and my shadow yearning for an unimaginable space. In the past several years, I often found my smartphone album were filled with the images in the forgotten corners.

I wonder: Who has been making frames in photography? Who has the power to reframe? What does it mean to unmake frames? Can we imagine a frame that could be, but is not yet?

Figure 6.3. Photography, R. Hadeer (2022).

Figure 6.4. Photography, R. Hadeer (2020).

Figure 6.5. Photography, R. Hadeer (2020).

With the curiosity to learn more about my own photography practice, I start to search for the readings on visual inquiry and educational research. I learn that the role of photography should not merely be a tool for the data collection to "reporting" for educational research under colonial framework; it is also deeply related to the "artistic, scientific, and everyday histories and practices within which it is already embroiled" (Vellanki, 2022, p. 135). What if I gave legitimate attention to my photographs that have emerged from my pure aesthetic intuition? What can I discover about self and the world? What possibilities would emerge? Building on the method of photo elicitation (Faulkner, 2018), I use a concept called *poetic photographic inquiry* to describe my poetic meditation on the medium of photography.

I am drawing on Rancière's (1991; 2013) philosophy on the poetic condition of human beings when I use the term "poetic" in *poetic photographic inquiry*. According to Rancière, every human being is a poetic being, but the operation of rhetoric is the absence of the poetic condition. "Rhetoric is speech in revolt against the poetic condition of the speaking being. It speaks in order to silence" (Rancière, 1991, p. 85). Rhetoric operates in order to prove others are wrong and bring a moment of silence. On the contrary, the poetic condition of human beings is seeking truth through the power of one's own inner intelligence instead of being schooled by an expert while acknowledging one will never achieve the larger and greater truth. In the methodology of *poetic photographic inquiry*, curation of a photo series presentation does not start from a top-down research question. Instead, it starts with photos that have already been created in everyday life without any attempt to answer a research question with pre-existing knowledge/assumptions. By radically legitimizing photos emerged in everyday life, *poetic photographic inquiry* meditates on the themes these photos are trying to convey, and how they can help us (un)learn more about the self and surroundings. Specifically, I use a website, https://slowphoto.weebly.com/, as a digital space to organize the photos in my smartphone, record my feelings, and materialize my embodying process of *poetic photographic inquiry*.

This website starts as a place for me to "play precisely because I am uncertain of what will happen" (Ulmer, 2017). As Koro-Ljungberg writes, "uncertainty, rawness, and creative chaos promoted by doing, engaging, collaborating, and reflecting through failure and unfinishedness (without constant and continual purification and 'cleaning' efforts) is conceptually life changing" (Koro-Ljungberg, 2016, p. 103). Gradually, I start to see themes emerge, and I put the photos in the subpages and categories, sometimes paired with written texts. Over the past several years, the website has slowly developed into a space that reflects my own poetic aesthetics and senses. It is a process that in which I am "untraining" (St. Pierre, 2016) myself from the framing that I have been trained to appreciate as beautiful, and finding my own way of seeing/framing the world.

When I was organizing the photos taken in distorted frames by my smartphone to capture the world from my own subaltern perspective (Spivak, 2015), I did not consider them as "art." Later, inspired by philosophers such as John Dewey, Jacques Rancière, and Elliot Eisner, I noticed that what I was doing could be called art (e.g., Dewey, 1934; Eisner, 2002; Rancièere, 2013). In a time of existential crisis in my life, art was and remains the only way my struggles, confusion, pain, and complex feelings are expressed in order to survive, to breathe, to continue to live and make meaning of my life. Art has become a survival technology.

Probably, art is education in and of itself, and as such, it is instrumental in processes of liberation for me. As bell hooks writes (2014, p. 59):

> I came to theory because I was hurting—the pain within me was so intense that I could not go on living. I came to theory desperate, wanting to comprehend— to grasp what was happening around me and within me. Most importantly, I wanted to make the hurt go away. I saw in theory then a location for healing.

bell hooks finds a way to survive in theory. For me, I find a way to survive in art. Art is my survival tool and my location for healing. To survive, to express myself, to make sense of the world during the existential crisis caused by the larger global context for Uyghur people's oppression, I come to art desperately. I have to think beyond the existing disciplinary boundaries and take up a "polydisciplinamory" stance (Loveless, 2019), crossing the borders of upheld categories to express myself through a bottom-up, inside-out, and more authentic way of bearing witness to reality. Thus, I have to think like an artist, which means going inward and creating the self continuously, even though it looks to be at odds with everything around it. The art I speak of here is no longer a skill set. It is a process of exploration and making sense of the world, a way of thinking, living, and being. Art has become my way of seeking personal emancipation.

After claiming my own photography-making practice as art because of the inspiration of philosophers' comments on the arts, I started to identify myself as an arts-based researcher, and I started to explore arts-based methodology in my doctoral program. Something I feel is unique about my journey to embrace aspects of my scholarly work as arts-based, which I believe distinguishes me from many other arts-based research scholars, is that I came to art because I was pushed to this way by the larger system and structure. I do not have any professional arts education background and started to learn it in my doctoral program. Students may come to arts-based research because they already have a formal arts education background, and when they attend doctoral program orientation, they notice "Oh, there is a category called arts-based research. I used to love it or I am always good at art. So let me do arts-based research." But for me, it is different. I identify as such, but I also transcend it.

I started my doctoral program by working with more social science-oriented research methods because I knew that I was not an artist, and I did not have any artist genes. Such a belief can be traced back to my schooling in China, and I remember the time I totally gave up on art during my boarding school. As an Uyghur originally from northwest China, I went to high school in the dislocated boarding school in the eastern part of the country. In the boarding school, Uyghur children are always expected to perform regional ethnic dance in front of the school official. But I never selected to perform Uyghur dances because I was never good at it.

As an Uyghur student in China, not knowing how to dance was my insecurity. School officials would always ask ethnic minorities for regional songs and dances. In the official Chinese textbooks, Uyghurs are always described as artistic people who are good at dancing, singing, sewing, and other kinds of arts. Throughout my schooling, I felt that I lacked the artistic skills necessary to project the image as an independent and authentic Uyghur comfortable in my own skin. Whenever there was a show on campus or in the city, Uyghur children would be on the frontline preparing something authentic. However, I always felt shame for not knowing how to dance like the other Uyghur girls who were skilled at it (Barros, Hadeer, & Gajasinghe, 2022). For me, traditional dances made them look cool, free, and empowered. All that I had to offer was my reputation as a stellar academic performer, a successfully integrated model minority in this predominantly Han Chinese region.

I intentionally befriended Uyghur classmates who were dance experts, hoping to add that "art language" to my repertoire. But I never became successful at it. Despite my hard work practicing dancing and multiple attempts to sign up for dancing performances, I never got a chance to be selected to participate in the dancing show when I was in boarding school. "Maybe I was not a good Uyghur after all," I thought. "Maybe I just did not have the artistic gene." Finally, I gave up trying to perform for others. In the bathroom, however, alone, I would move my body in front of the mirror. Dancing became something uniquely mine—clumsy, imperfect, rhythmically disjointed, but mine. During the boarding school, I subconsciously formed a habit of only dancing when I was alone. For myself.

Since then, I have avoided associating myself with art. I was convinced that I wasn't born with any dancing genes, and I didn't have any artistic talent. After high school, during my undergraduate study in another city in the Eastern part of China, when ethnic minorities are still asked to perform Uyghur dances or songs, I naturally walked away from invitations. I accepted the hard truth that I did not want to admit: I was not born to be an artist, and I was not a good Uyghur.

As I recall my memory in the boarding school in China (Barros, Hadeer, & Gajasinghe, 2022), I realized that the dance I performed alone for myself in the bathroom in my boarding school in China was art. That might not be a good dance from the school officials' aesthetic perspective on what represents a "good" Uyghur, but it was my genuine struggle to negotiate my true self with the authorities' expectations. That very process of moving my body in my own way was my art. Definitions of "art" and "good art" are not defined by outside discourse, delinking from dominant and traditional ways of distribution of senses (e.g., Mignolo & Vazquez, 2013).

Figure 6.6. Photography, R. Hadeer (2020).

References

Barros, S. R., Hadeer, R., & Gajasinghe, K. (2022). Confabulating research: Performing memory-work as inquiry. *International Review of Qualitative Research, 15*(1), 21–41.

Bovingdon, G. (2004). *Autonomy in Xinjiang: Han nationalist imperatives and Uyghur discontent.* East-West Center, Washington.

Crowley, C. B., Hadeer, R., & Yu, M. (2021). Rethinking teacher education for ethnic diversity in China. *Educational Studies*, 1–21.

Dewey, J. (1934). *Art as experience.* Minton, Balch.

Dwyer, A. M. (2005). *The Xinjiang conflict: Uyghur identity, language policy, and political discourse.* East-West Center, Washington.

Eisner, E. W. (2002). *The arts and the creation of mind.* Yale University Press.

Faulkner, S. L. (2018). Poetic inquiry: Poetry as/in/for social research. In P. Leavy (Ed.), *Handbook of arts-based research* (pp. 208–230). The Guilford Press.

hooks, b. (2014). *Teaching to transgress.* Routledge.

Koro-Ljungberg, M. (2016). *Reconceptualizing qualitative research: Methodologies without methodology.* SAGE.

Loveless, N. (2019). *How to make art at the end of the world.* Duke University Press.

Mignolo, W., & Vazquez, R. (2013). Decolonial aesthesis: Colonial wounds/decolonial healings–Social text. *Social Text Periscope: an Online Journal.* Retrieved December 15, 2019.

Rancière, J. (1991). *The ignorant schoolmaster* (Vol. 1). Stanford University Press.

Rancière, J. (2013). *Aisthesis: Scenes from the aesthetic regime of art.* Verso Books.

Shichor, Y. (2005). Blow up: Internal and external challenges of Uyghur separatism and Islamic radicalism to Chinese rule in Xinjiang. *Asian Affairs: An American Review, 32*(2), 119–136

Spivak, G. C. (2015). Can the subaltern speak? In *Colonial discourse and post-colonial theory* (pp. 66–111). Routledge.

St. Pierre E. A. (2016). Untraining educational researchers. *Research in Education, 96*(1), 6–11.

Teng.X, & Ma,X. (2005). China's preferential policy to minority nationalities in higher education and education equality. *Journal of Ethno-National Studies, 5*, 2002. http://en.cnki.com.cn/Article_en/CJFDTOTAL-MZYJ200505002.htm

Ulmer, J. B. (2017). Composing techniques: Choreographing a post-qualitative writing practice. *Qualitative Inquiry*, online advance publication, 1–9.

Vellanki, V. (2022). Shifting the frame: Theoretical and methodological explorations of photography in educational research. *Cultural Studies ↔ Critical Methodologies, 22*(2), 132–142.

Zhao, Z. (2011). Empowerment in a socialist egalitarian agenda: Minority women in China's higher education system. *Gender and Education, 23*(4), 431–445.

Zhou, M. (2001). The politics of bilingual education in the People's Republic of China since 1949. *Bilingual Research Journal, 25*(1–2), 147–171.

SEVEN

Here We Go Again: Three Narratives of Struggle to Disrupt Racial Dominance in Education Spaces

Rae Fox-Charles, Thong Vang, and Asha Omar

Here We Go Again: Three Narratives of Struggle to
Disrupt Racial Dominance in Education Spaces

THE THREE AUTHORS OF THIS paper are all people of color who came together in a doctoral seminar on culturally relevant pedagogy in the fall of 2020. Throughout the sessions, we found ourselves ruminating over shared frustrations. We were disappointed at how whiteness prohibited class conversations from delving into deeper theoretical analysis. The perspectives of white educators dominated our class discourse and consistently pulled focus. Additionally, the group found it impossible to discuss asset-based pedagogies without acknowledging issues of race, culture, social justice, and oppression. Ignorance and white fragility manifested weekly in breakout rooms and full class meetings despite the instructor's best efforts. We found ourselves asking questions that no one else was asking. Our shared feelings of isolation brought us together to ask ourselves, "Why?"

In sharing our experiences with one another, we quickly realized that our unique perspectives as BIPOC educators were driving us to think about pedagogy, practice, and diversity differently than our peers. We subscribed to alternate epistemologies that rendered the insidiousness of whiteness visible to us alone (Yancy, 2014). Our assessments of culturally relevant pedagogy (CRP) and other asset-based pedagogies were significantly impacted by what we experienced as students and continue to experience presently as educators. For us, the question was not about what these pedagogies could do for *them*—meaning our students of color—but what impact these pedagogies would have on *us* and *ours* as members of these communities. What did it mean to bridge, and what were we bridging to? Wouldn't it be better to spend our efforts eradicating white supremacy instead of seeking validation of our own ways of knowing and being? Where is the line between relating, appropriating, and mocking student culture for the sake of academic achievement?

We found ourselves outsiders, and every class risked doing us harm. We have written this paper as a way of healing. We have written this paper to acknowledge the efficacy of our ancestral teaching practices. We were and are doing this work already—more effectively. Generations of BIPOC educators already understood the importance of validating students' cultural, racial, linguistic, and ethnic identities because the world outside of their classroom would not. We continue in their legacy and share the following three individual narratives because we recognize that "the socially situated epistemic insights of people of color are *indispensable*" (Yancy, 2014, p. 48).

Findings and Analysis

We reflect and share our lived experiences as doctoral students, specifically focusing on our participation in the fall semester of 2020 when each of us enrolled in a course on Culturally Relevant Pedagogy. While narrative inquiry focuses on understanding and generating questions from individual people's experiences, it also considers justifying narrative inquiry on different levels: personal, practice, and social levels (Clandinin & Huber, 2010). Drawing on studies that take up narrative inquiry as a collaborative process of sharing, shaping, and interpreting our stories and lives (Clandinin & Connelly, 2000; Clandinin & Huber, 2010), we reflect and theorize our experiences and memories to contextualize our analysis toward generative dialogue. This process includes theorizing on each of our narratives and cross-reading one another's narratives.

Author Positionality

Asha is a biracial Somali American who currently serves as an equity teacher for Anti-Racist Elementary School. Her work in the school focuses on building solidarity with adults and youth to foster spaces of racial healing and resist oppressive practices that limit Black joy. She has over 8 years of teaching experience and identifies as a scholar/activist (Fine, 2018) to employ critical research as a means of improving the school community.

Thong is a HMoob[1] American scholar and was a child refugee. His family resettled in the United States due to the Secret War in Laos. He is currently involved in HMoob ethnic studies curriculum development for the State of California. His research looks at ways HMoob ways of knowing and being are implemented in school and informal learning spaces.

Rae, is a Black American scholar currently researching Black education, narrative, dance pedagogy and social justice education. She currently serves as an Arts & Equity Specialist for the Minnesota Department of Education where she is able to redefine culturally responsive curriculum, practices, and policies throughout the state. Ultimately, she seeks to synthesize her diverse experiences into a career as a consultant, educator, author, and independent researcher.

Personal Narratives

Asha

Part of my position as an equity teacher at Anti-Racist Elementary School is to facilitate meaningful spaces with staff to engage them in exercises that will build their critical consciousness. One of the ways that I have chosen to do this is by sending out a bi-weekly newsletter with resources such as books, podcasts, embodied exercises, and other teaching materials to provide opportunities to build awareness of different socio-political issues. I then use the readings provided in the previous weeks as a common foundation on which to build when we come together on Wednesdays for our Justice Circles. Justice Circles are based on Indigenous and Afrocentric ways of coming together as a community to do restorative practice (Hand et al., 2012). This work has never been done in a professional development setting like the one that I am facilitating with the teachers and which has now become a part of the school schedule. Two times a month teachers know that they will be engaging in this work in community with their peers to build their socio-political consciousness and, one hopes, begin to show up better for our predominantly Black and Brown student body. Up to this point, the circles have been interracial and inclusive of all staff members employed at the elementary school. So far, they have been going well. Teachers and administrators have been coming together to share stories of their experiences with belonging, racialization, and what they have on their plates for building a sense of unity and understanding with each other. This past Wednesday was different. I was facilitating a circle around two chapters from *My Grandmother's Hands* (Menakem, 2018) with the prompt: "Think about the earliest, *strongest* memory you have, that made you conscious of your race."

I shared two deeply personal stories, the first about being excluded from an entire class birthday party in kindergarten and realizing it was because I was the only Black student in the class. The second was in first grade, when a classmate asked why my skin was so dirty and informed me that her dad told her that Black people are this color because they don't wash themselves well, so I went home and scrubbed my skin until it got raw. The other people of color in the group shared similar stories that reflected a time when they were made aware that people perceived them in a negative way. These stories were all from early childhood memories, and each shared how they informed them about how to move differently in certain spaces. Traumatic! The white teachers in the circle shared stories about the first time they realized that there were other races. A select few shared stories of their awareness of what it means to be white; all of these stories were drawn from their college experience. This was a very different theme, a consciousness of race versus a consciousness of being white. I also noticed that two Black women in the circle decided not to share. They turned their cameras off, muted themselves, and left the call as soon as I closed the circle.

I've been there. I know that feeling without asking. It's the feeling of doing emotional labor and exposing your traumas for someone else to sympathize with your pain. It's not healing, it's not transformative, it's for white consumption, and I completely understand why they decided they didn't want to go there. Fair enough. As Black, Brown, and Indigenous people, we have experienced the violence, hatred, and overall oppression that racialization brings, while white people have the luxury of ignoring it. We have engaged in these conversations from a young age and have processed what this means in our bodies. White people have not. White people need to consider: What does it mean to be deprived of or blissfully unaware of experiences that allow you insight into your racialization? And how can you be in community with people who have had endless experience?

This reflection, after holding that space at work, has me wondering if engaging in this racial healing work is productive in groups that are interracial. It does not seem to be healing for the Black, Brown, and Indigenous people in the room. We all have a unique understanding of the pervasiveness of whiteness, and sitting in spaces and listening to people who are just beginning their journey is not helpful. It again recenters whiteness, and we are left trying to push them to a critical point rather than thinking of ways to transform our own practice. My hope is that this work can be done in community with all teachers, but the continuous recentering of whiteness is not productive and is something that I am deeply against.

Considering the course Culturally Relevant Pedagogy (CRP), I see many parallels in my experience of trying to engage in critical work with my white peers. The conversations never got to a point where I felt understood or that I was gaining something for my practice. It was once more relating the text to my lived experiences and my white peers theorizing through different texts. While I am fond of Gloria Ladson Billings's work and the work surrounding asset-based pedagogies, who are we trying to heal? Who is benefiting from these conversations? Haymes (1997) states that as a Black community we need to develop a pedagogy that would allow Black people to engage in ways that reconnect with their historical, social, and political origins. I would have liked to spend time processing how communities of color already do this work, rather than trying to convince white folks why the work is important. On the rare occasion that Rae, Thong, and myself were able to discuss course literature regarding our cultural, epistemological, and ancestral backgrounds, we were able to consider the ways in which we grew up around CRP. We discussed how CRP was used by our families over the years and considered how this could translate into a classroom setting. It was the most rewarding part of the class by far.

Thong

My experience in our culturally relevant coursework felt incomplete. I was confused about why we had semester-long discussions about our refusal to imagine beyond the current teaching and learning practices we see in schools. Students were bewildered by the limits of our existing institutions, hindering our ability to enact CRP. I saw the resistance to moving beyond surface-level conversations in our culturally relevant course as the resurgence of the dominant culture in a space that was supposed to disrupt it. While this is not surprising, it certainly defeats the purpose of the course.

Silences, undisrupted by long pauses and stares, recenter dominant white culture in race-related discussions (Kraehe, 2015; Mazzei, 2008; Nichols & Wacek, 2019; Pollock, 2004). To break the tension of awkwardness is to move away from the uncomfortable topic, a much-needed conversation, to a more comfortable one that maintains the status quo. I experienced this both in the courses I have taken and in discussions with members of my community—for instance, in talks on HMoob language and culture class. The parallel here is the refusal of pluralistic expressions of HMoobness, such as customs, histories, regions, and sub-dialects, such as that of HMoob Leeg people's existence within HMoob language and culture curricula.

One of the most common questions and critiques of asset-based pedagogies is "Yes, but how do we do it?" (Ladson-Billings, 2006), which speaks to the nature of scripted curriculum in U.S. public education and teacher education systems. It declares a need for standardization of everything. The unwillingness to see beyond what has been done has to do with the critiques of CRP—specifically, that CRP cannot be implemented because there "isn't enough time" and because teachers do not have enough knowledge of another culture to include it in their teachings. Worse is tokenizing, simplifying cultures to what we see today in schools, which in some way could have been a genuine step toward recognizing cultures in classroom spaces. Yet cultures and people from non-dominant communities are limited in school curricula to a day or a month (i.e., Black History Month, Asian American History Month, and HMoob American Day). However, CRP suggests that students come into the classroom with their cultures and languages everyday (Ladson-Billings, 2006).

In my personal experience, I have witnessed HMoob language and culture teachers exhibiting what Flores and Rosa (2015) referred to as raciolinguistic ideologies. It is where educators often cite their lack of knowledge of the other HMoob dialects and traditions. At times, they downplay the number of students who speak marginalized dialects, stating that the current HMoob curricula reflect the majority-speaking community and therefore justify their teachings approaches, even when there are no statistics on the distribution of HMoob dialect speakers. This intragroup subordination and erasure of other HMoob histories, dialects, and cultures occur when our own people refuse to acknowledge our multiplicity. While there is value in presenting a united front as a marginalized group, curricula that include only one community's history, language, and customs tend to exclude those who most need to feel included.

This assumption that we need a homogenous curriculum is laced with biases and misrepresentations. We see here that HMoob language and culture programs are systemically simplified by the U.S. public education system to what is "teachable." Systematically it positions marginalized communities against each other for superiority, so that there could only be one HMoob language and culture curriculum. This demand created competition among marginalized communities and leaders to homogenize their knowledge and their people's history for the system. Despite this, HMoob educators know in their hearts that HMoob is many and pluralistic. HMoob speakers often engage in trans-lingual and trans-dialect conversations that are strengthened through their multi-dialect relationships. I draw this parallel connection between the conversations I have heard in HMoob language and culture programs and those I experienced in my CRP course, because they are both connected to systematic approaches to education. As a person who has experienced systematic marginalization, I am tired and confused about why it is so hard to imagine beyond what has previously been done, while also recognizing the energy required to go up against systemic barriers.

The parallel connection between the discussions in our culturally relevant course and the conversations on HMoob language and culture classes both maintains and continues to limit us to the current system, which curtails our imagining of what could be for our learning community and HMoob language and culture curricula. The lasting thought for me is that while CRP is a grand theory, it had its time being a buzzword. Using CRP in conversations has undoubtedly made educators and schools appear more "aware," yet educators perpetuate harm by not enacting CRP in their practices. As a HMoob student, I believe that CRP and other asset-based pedagogies have much to offer and will continue to inform the work I hope to accomplish with my community. However, without a critical examination of CRP for educators of color, they may enact "CRP" that further alienates and erases the history and knowledge of their kin and other relatives.

Rae

> *I find myself sitting silent and willing my face to not give me away. I am willing my eyes to not go to the side. I'm willing my lips to keep an exasperated sigh from escaping. I'm willing my fingers to remain away from the keyboard. Now is not the time to unmute me and explain, nor will I give in to the pettiness of*

private messaging my homegirl in the other breakout room. We're not doing this today. I'm not doing this today, not again. This isn't what I came for!

I recall this inner monologue from a session of the doctoral seminar on culturally relevant pedagogy (CRP) that I took this semester. I frequently still feel how I felt then. It is how I and my BIPOC femme colleagues often feel in academia's supposedly racially conscious spaces: *stifled, exhausted, bound.* Instead of biting my tongue, I'm writing this paper to declare that we are tired. We carry the burden of vigilantly calling out, defending against, and convincing others of the dangerous insidiousness of whiteness whenever and wherever it appears. It does not matter what we hoped to gain or learn from being in these spaces. That work will have to wait, for we are obligated to do the work of dealing with whiteness first. Sometimes whiteness comes forth from one of my well-intentioned classmates' mouths, as it did that day. Other times it sits half-hidden in the corner of the classroom. I find it most shocking when whiteness leaps out from a page of required reading.

I discovered Gloria Ladson-Billings and her canonical piece, "Toward a Theory of Culturally Relevant Pedagogy" (1995) during my first year of graduate school. Like bell hooks, "I came to theory because I was hurting . . . I came to theory desperate, wanting to comprehend—to grasp what was happening around and within me" (hooks, 1994, p. 59). Pieces like Ladson-Billings's (1995)—pieces that advocated for the dignity and intellect of Black children, whether they demanded justice, abolition, or merely reform—gave me hope and were unquestioningly absorbed into my own developing theoretical framework. My research would be dedicated to the discovery and popularization of a culturally relevant way of teaching dance—a liberatory dance pedagogy—one with transferable principles for how to best serve Black children in various educational contexts and content areas. CRP became the buzzword that I tacked onto my scholarship in order to legitimize myself and my work. Yet the more I studied, the more I encountered culturally relevant pedagogy and all its offshoots, variations, and developments, and the more I became curious. Actually, I became increasingly suspicious that no one, including myself, really knew what CRP was or how to implement it with integrity.

This is how I recently found myself enrolled in a course dedicated to culturally relevant pedagogy. I wanted to dissect the foundational texts. I wanted to track the theory's refinement over time. I wanted to strategize how to learn from its successful implementations as well as its failures. Unfortunately,

I experienced little of this. I came to understand how, despite its three pillars of academic achievement, cultural competence, and sociopolitical consciousness (Ladson-Billings, 2006), CRP and its related asset-based pedagogies were more often manifested as technologies of whiteness (Leonardo & Zembylas, 2013) than effective tools for the educational liberation that Black and other culturally marginalized children so desperately need(ed). In part due to theoretical fissures or the lack of criticality when put into practice (Ladson-Billings, 2006), and in part due to white educators' difficulty in recognizing and relinquishing their own stake in whiteness, the theory of CRP itself became tarnished, thanks to this one teleological flaw.

Culturally relevant pedagogy was never meant to redefine "academic success." Ladson-Billings' concept "came as a result of [her] desire to challenge deficit paradigms" that had come to characterize Black students (1995, p. 472). CRP was developed to show that Black children could be made to achieve in school. Ladson-Billings clearly makes a point to shift her analysis from the "school failure of African American students" to "examin[ing] academic success among African American students" (1995, p. 275)—distinguishing her work from the current body of literature. The theory of CRP was never meant to address the systemic problems that made schooling a site of such suffering for Black children in the first place.

The difference here is a small but consequential one. By locating the problem in schools, researchers create the opportunity to address that system and potentially redefine the benchmarks of academic success. We are able to alter which ways of knowing and whose knowledge, behavior, and creativity gets validated. However, if students' relatively poor achievement is pinned on Black students themselves, or even their teachers, then student failure has more to do with individual moral failings than with systemic oppression. In effect, by asserting that Black student achievement was a consequence of how these students were being taught, Ladson-Billings minimizes the systemic nature of the achievement gap. She fails to acknowledge the reality that Black students are failing by design, and no fault of their own. Knowing full well that more often than not "students' academic success came at the expense of their cultural and psychosocial well-being," she misses the opportunity to completely denounce whiteness and its construction of success. Consequently, whiteness has continued to corrupt theorizations of asset-based pedagogies to this day (Ohito, 2020, p. 215).

I could no longer engage with these frameworks in the same way once it became apparent that the purpose of so-called, asset-based pedagogies was not to disrupt the hegemonic forces in our schools that work to ensure that whiteness is conflated with success, intelligence, and achievement, but to instead pass minoritized students through the assimilatory machine of P–12 schooling. My goals for the course shifted from a desire to implement to a desire to observe and understand how whiteness had so infiltrated what seemed at first to be anti-racist frameworks. When I began to listen for what was really being theorized in these learning spaces rather than what I wanted to hear, I noticed the affect of white fragility popping up everywhere (Leonardo & Zembylas, 2013). White teachers in diverse school settings complained of being too burned out to incorporate asset-based teaching into any self-reflective praxis. White administrators complained that recognizing the value of Black ways of knowing rather than punishing them would put their jobs into precarity. These white graduate students and teacher-educators continually centered themselves in discussions of how they could do better by BIPOC students—more concerned with protecting their image of themselves than serving students.

Recognizing myself as a Black femme body that is "always already racially historicized, sexualized, physicalized, and demonized" even before I'd entered a classroom, I realized I was faced with a choice (Alexander, 2005, p. 250). I could submit to the racism of our class discourses—like a Mammy—hoping that if I were gentle enough, spoke kindly and quietly enough as I endured the harm of patiently suffering through these conversations, then they might begin to shift. My colleagues would be inspired to take these pedagogies up differently; Black students would be treated differently; my Blackness could exist in these educational spaces differently. I could raise *these* white folks to be better.

Alternatively, I could forfeit my share of this legacy. I could refuse to participate in the particularly feminized Black experience that demanded so much of my Black-womanness. I could speak out, correct, and condemn whiteness whenever its specter became visible and clouded conversation. I could risk the backlash of becoming the class's angry Black woman. If I raised my fists and raised my voice, no, I wouldn't be Mammy, but I would still be Peaches[2]— dismissed and demonized. This second strategy would preserve my self-respect while risking my reputation. Sometimes the louder you yell, the less (white) folks are willing to listen. Black feminists have long warned that "the psychological [and professional, and personal, and physical, and spiritual] toll of being a Black woman and the difficulties this presents in reaching political consciousness and doing political work can never be underestimated" (Combahee River Collective, 1977/2000, p. 266). Education is always political work, and work that has to be done. I could take whiteness by the hand, put its burdens on my back, and long-sufferingly believe that one day we would make it to the promised land. Or I could seethe, and rage—wearing myself out trying to prove how much the work isn't mine to do. Either way, my fate remained bound to this legacy, "the outgrowth of countless generations of personal sacrifice, militancy, and work by [my Black] mothers and sisters" (Combahee River Collective, 1977/2000, p. 262).

I am no longer subscribing to cultural relevance/response/sustenance in my scholarship or my teaching because it is not enough and because it is too much. The field of education must go where Ladson-Billings and others are urging us, while recognizing that this will still not be far enough. Fordham and Ogbu (1986), Ladson-Billings (1995), Gay (2010, 2013), Paris (2012), and others' advice for how BIPOC students ought to be taught and researched offer marked improvement from where American education started. Gay's emphasis on leveraging student diversity (2013) and Paris's insistence that we must sustain cultures (2012; Paris & Alim, 2014) both represent better frameworks for teaching diverse students than we had before. Yet these frameworks ask us to relate, sustain, and respond to cultures—actions of reform, not revolution. I can no longer allow myself to be amongst educators pacified by asset-based pedagogies that cannot offer the abolition that BIPOC and other marginalized students need (Ohito, 2020; Love, 2019; Shange, 2019). Asset-based pedagogies are not radical enough to eradicate the whiteness continuing to operate in our schools—dominating our ideas and skewing our understanding of justice, success, and progress. It is too much to ask that I sit in this course, in these types of supposedly woke racial-justice-oriented educational spaces, and be mammified or worse.

Perhaps, there is a third choice that better describes the work I have chosen to do instead. Then and now, I find myself trying to sit in discernment—to listen without reaction, without judgment, without any investment in acknowledging whiteness at all. Once I recognized my own agency in determining how, when, and why I engage in this work, I found another way—one grounded in redressing Black educators' and students' needs first and foremost. We are agents, not assets to be cashed in by the bank white supremacy. Black women might never escape our legacy of labor, but we can labor in love, in community, and toward liberation.

Closing Thoughts

These three narratives raise important concerns about cultivating critical spaces at a graduate level. Each narrative holds themes of emotional labor, intellectual labor, and an overall feeling of not being seen within the classroom. What does it mean for graduate students of color to be trained CRP? How much of CRP's teaching and theories vary from what they already know? If we are already doing the work of our ancestors, we are doing CRP. Too often in higher education we are then being taught the work in a way that has been so theorized for White academic consumption that it is rendered unfamiliar to us. One way to invest in CRP and asset-based pedagogies is to commit to the communities from which this knowledge came. Understand these pedagogies as they already exist in our communities, rather than purporting to reimagine education for students of color. We encourage the development of courses and critical spaces that allow students of color to expand their epistemologies in healing and productive ways rather than burdening them with the obligation to facilitate the education of their white peers.

Scholarly Significance

This paper contributes not only to teacher education research but also serves as a resource for the communities involved in supporting teachers who are pursuing inclusive and socially just education in their daily practice. It uplifts voices that are often silenced in these spaces and highlights pitfalls to be avoided, The implications for graduate and education programs would be to look at creating more outlets to address students' concerns on courses they have taken in order to improve their learning outcomes, and by asking the question, "How do we decenter whiteness in academic courses so that BIPOC scholars do not feel the institutional pressures to do intellectual and emotional labor for their peers' consumption?"

Notes

1. Groups of people within our community are distinguished by our customs and dialects. The term HMoob, with capitalized "HM," is an iteration that comes from combining the "H" in Hmoob dlawb (White) dialect and "M" from the Moob leeg hab Moob ntsuab (Leng and Green) dialects. HMoob dlawb, Moob leeg, and Moob Ntsuab are major dialects spoken by the HMoob community the United States. This paper utilizes HMoob (Thao, 2019; Xiong, 2018).

2. "Four Women" (1966) is a song written and performed by Black jazz artist Nina Simone in which she monologues from the perspectives of four main stereotypes of Black womanhood: Miss Sara, the Mammy; Saffronia, the Tragic Mulatto; Sweet Thing, the Jezebel; and Peaches, the Angry Black Woman.

References

Alexander, B. K. (2005) Embracing the teachable moment: The Black gay body in the classroom as embodied text. In E. Patrick Johnson & M. G. Henderson (Eds.), *Black queer studies: A critical anthology* (pp. 249–265).

Clandinin, D. J., & Connelly, F. M. (2000). *Narrative inquiry: Experience and story in qualitative research.* San Francisco: Jossey-Bass.

Clandinin, D. J., & Huber, J. (2010). Narrative inquiry. In B. McGaw, E. Baker, & P. P. Peterson (Eds.), *International encyclopedia of education* (3rd ed.). Elsevier.

Combahee River Collective (1977/2000). A Black feminist statement. In J. James & T. D. Sharpley-Whiting (Eds.), *The Black feminist reader.* Blackwell.

Fine, M. (2018). *Just research in contentious times: Widening the methodological imagination.* New York, NY: Teachers College Press.

Flores, N., & Rosa, J. (2015). Undoing appropriateness: Raciolinguistic ideologies and language diversity in education. *Harvard Educational Review, 85*(2), 149–301.

Fordham, S., & Ogbu, J.U. (1986). Black students' school success: Coping with the "burden of 'acting white'". *The Urban Review, 18,* 176-206.

Gay, G. (2010). *Culturally responsive teaching: Theory, research, and practice* (2nd ed.). Teachers College Press.

Gay, G. (2013). Teaching to and through cultural diversity. *Curriculum Inquiry, 43*(1), 48–70.

Hand, C., Hankes, J., & House, T. (2012). Restorative Justice: The Indigenous justice system. *Contemporary Justice Review, 12*(4), 449–467. doi: 10.1080/10282580.2012.734576

hooks, b. (1994). *Teaching to transgress: Education as the practice of freedom.* Routledge.

Haymes, S. (1997). Black culture identity, white consumer culture, and the politics of difference. *African American Review, 31*(1), 125–128. doi:10.2307/3042187

Kraehe, A. M. (2015). Sounds of silence: Race and emergent counter-narratives of art teacher identity. *Studies in Art Education, 56*(3), 199–213. doi: 10.1080/00393541.2015.11518963

Ladson-Billings, G. (1995). Toward a theory of culturally relevant pedagogy. *American Educational Research Journal, 32*(3), 465–491.

Ladson-Billings, G. (2006). Yes, but how do we do it? Practicing culturally relevant pedagogy. In J. Landsman & C. W. Lewis (Eds.), *White teachers/diverse classrooms: A guide to building inclusive schools, promoting high expectations, and eliminating racism* (pp. 29–42). Stylus.

Leonardo, Z., & Zembylas, M. (2013). Whiteness as technology of affect: Implications for educational praxis. *Equity & Excellence in Education, 46*(1), 150–165. https://doi.org/10.1080/1066 5684.2013.750539

Love, B. L. (2019) *We want to do more than survive: Abolitionist teaching and the pursuit of educational freedom*. Beacon Press.

Mazzei, L. A. (2008) Silence speaks: Whiteness revealed in the absence of voice. *Teaching and Teacher Education, 24*(1), 1125–1136. doi: 10.1016/j.tate.2007.02.009

McCarty, T., & Lee, T. (2014). Critical culturally sustaining/revitalizing pedagogy and Indigenous education sovereignty. *Harvard Educational Review, 84*(1), 101–124.

Menakem, R. (2018). *My grandmother's hands*. Central Recovery Press.

Nichols, M. D., & Wacek, J. A. (2019). Frangible Whiteness: Teaching race in the context of White fragility. In P. Bolton, C. L. Smith, & L. Bebout (Eds.), *Teaching with tension: Race, resistance, and reality in the classroom* (pp. 239–254). Northwestern University Press.

Ohito, Esther O. (2020). "The creative aspect woke me up": Awakening to multimodal essay composition as a fugitive literacy practice. *English Education, 52*(3), 186–222.

Paris, D. (2012). Culturally sustaining pedagogy: A needed change in stance, terminology, and practice. *Educational Researcher, 41*(3), 93–97.

Paris, D., & Alim, H. S. (2014). What are we seeking to sustain through culturally sustaining pedagogy? A loving critique forward. *Harvard Educational Review, 84*(1), 85–100.

Pollock, M. (2004). *Colormute: Race talk dilemmas in an American school*. Princeton University Press.

Shange, S. (2019). *Progressive dystopia: Abolition, anthropology, and race in the new San Francisco*. Duke University Press.

Thao, A. (2019). The emerging preference for "HMoob" as a term of self-identification. *Expanding Access Quarterly*. https://blogs.extension.wisc.edu/oaic/files/2020/09/F001.Hmong-to-HMoob. pdf?fbclid=IwAR3NTUQDJ_7BIaTzdBeD3jOT510KnLMttiSD4nGx4UykqmC-yGcSw51M EDU

Xiong, X. (2018). Hmoobness: Hmoob (Hmong) youth and their perceptions of Hmoob language in a small town in the Midwest (Publication No. 10788367). Doctoral dissertation, The University of Minnesota, Twin Cities. Proquest.

Yancy, G. (2014). White gazes: What it feels like to be an essence. In Lee, E. S., *Living alterities: Phenomenology, embodiment, and race* (pp. 43–64). State University of New York Press.

EIGHT

Culturally Competent Teachers in Action in an Urban-Multicultural Classroom through a Qualitative Research Lens

Benedict Adams

Philosophical Foundations of American Education

IN ORDER TO UNDERSTAND THE deeper fundamentals of teacher learning, diversity, equity, and inclusion in teacher identity development, it is essential to conceptualize the philosophical underpinnings of the American education system. Philosophy is one of the fundamental subjects (along with history and psychology) that forms the fundamental underpinnings upon which the practice of education rests (Ryan, Cooper, & Bolick, 2019). Philosophy asks the fundamental questions of existence, knowledge, and learning, and explores what and how these can be shared with future generations. In light of this background, it is important to reveal that the U.S. educational system is founded on four schools of thought: perennialism, essentialism, romanticism, and progressivism (Ryan, Cooper, & Bolick, 2019). Thus, it is these domains that influence teacher learning and educators' socially mediated process of their identity-work and development.

Perennialism has its foundations in the writings of Plato, which view truth and human nature as constant, unchanging, and objective. Therefore, searching for the truth means exchanging ideas until clarity or light is reached. In this way, education develops in a person the mental discipline and rationality necessary in searching for truth. Perennialists see the school's role as teaching disciplined knowledge in order to promote intellectual richness of the mind. Education, for them, develops the personal mental discipline and rationality that are essential to searching for truths that help humans avoid being dominated by instincts. Likewise, the teacher's role is the development of the intellect through a teacher-directed instructional approach that fosters these fundamental skills. Nevertheless, perennialist teachers see their role as passing on greater truths to the next generation as effectively and forcefully as possible. Therefore, students need to be pushed to their limits, because life is very demanding.

Essentialism. This philosophical discourse grew in the 1930s as a reaction to what was seen as an overemphasis on a child-centered approach to education. Based on both Aristotle's realism and Plato's idealism, Essentialists believe that children should learn only what is essential, along with the method and skills prescribed to transmit it. Thus, the aim of education is to teach the youth life essentials they will need to become responsible citizens in this modern dispensation. To realize this goal, schools need to focus on the established disciplines that they said were repositories of organized knowledge (Ryan, Cooper, & Bolick, 2019). In this way, schools are places where kids learn and teachers become authorities for the essentials, and thus it is the teachers' responsibility to find out what is useful and to make sure that students learn it.

Romanticism. Also known as naturalism, this philosophy is based on the writings of Jean-Jacques Rousseau, an 18th-century Swiss-French thinker who believed that children are born good and pure, but that society corrupts them. Hence, they need to be protected from the evils of society (Ryan, Cooper, & Bolick, 2019) by being isolated from society for as long as possible. Since we all have a natural sense of awe, education should promote this natural sense; therefore, the Romantics believe that the teachers' job is to respond to the children's interests and curiosities as they arise, and not to force the learning of subjects that are not of interest to them. There can be no definitive curriculum, no tests, and no formal classes. Thus, Romantic teachers explore children's interests, satisfy their curiosities, and further steer their enthusiasm for learning in class.

Progressivism. This philosophy came to prominence in the 1920s and was inspired by the political and social Progressive Movement of the time. Drawing from the ideas of Dewey, progressivism viewed nature as being in flux and ever-changing; as a consequence, knowledge must continually be redefined and rediscovered to keep up with that change (Ryan, Cooper, & Bolick, 2019). For Progressives, the place to begin an education is with the student rather than with the subject matter. Thus, teachers identify each student's interests and concerns and attempt to shape problems around them. Teachers simply intellectually guide and facilitate the problem-solving process. They focus on teaching *how* to think rather than *what* to think. Unlike romantic educators, who see the world as a negative influence on students, Progressives see the society as integral to a student's life and schools as small societies where students learn as they live.

Progressivism and the influence of psychological theories-constructivism

Since the early 20th century, educational practices have been influenced by the discipline of psychology, especially cognitive psychology, which has played a prominent role. They drew on Piaget, Vygotsky, and Bruner, who discovered more about how people learn to think and solve problems, an approach that led to new ways for educators to teach. Constructivism took center stage; "Thus new information to be internalized by learners must be integrated into the learners' preexisting knowledge base" (Ryan, Cooper, & Bolick, p. 296). Similarly, knowledge cannot be transmitted directly from teachers to learners, but is rather constructed by learners and later reconstructed as new information becomes available. Thus, instead of seeing students as vessels waiting to be filled with knowledge, constructivists view them as actively engaged in meaning-making. Teachers therefore need to create learning situations wherein students can build their own knowledge rather than sit idly.

Constructivist identity and the Port Royal Experiment

Some analysts and historians conceptualize the identity transformative experience of constructivist teacher analogously to the Port Royal Experiment program (Parten, 2016). Port Royal, a program that began during the American Civil War, witnessed former African slaves successfully working on land abandoned by planters. In 1861, the Union captured the Sea Islands off the coast of South Carolina and their main harbor, Port Royal. The White residents fled, leaving behind about 10,000 Black slaves. Several teachers and private northern charity organizations stepped in to help the former slaves become self-sufficient. Through education and identity curricular approaches, the African Americans demonstrated their ability to work on the land efficiently and live independently of White control. They assigned themselves daily tasks for cotton growing and spent their extra time cultivating their own crops, fishing, hunting, and learning how to read and write (Parten, 2016). By selling their surplus crops, the locals were able to acquire small pieces of property. This transformative experience of a hard-work ethic, along with their strong motivation to attain basic education, has been widely admired.

Do teachers' identity and their critical philosophical approach matter?

As shown in the literature, this fundamental question has been asked since the Reconstruction Era, and research has thus been clear that teachers' identity and their philosophy in action matter (Danielewicz, 2014; Dewey, 1964; Sleeter, 2013; Ryan, Cooper, & Bolick, 2019). Perennialist teachers manifest their identity as the transmitters of knowledge to develop mental discipline and rationality in their search for truth (Ryan, Cooper, & Bolick, 2019). Likewise, essentialist teachers' approach manifests that there exists a critical core of information and skills that an educated person must have. Progressivism, which leads to Constructivism, sees students as actively engaged in meaning-making. Thus, teachers are seen as facilitators of learning situations rather than observers of students as empty tins to be filled with knowledge.

The rationale for this study was to explore how the teachers negotiated their identities and used culturally responsive skills as advocates for students in an urban multicultural classroom. In the course of a year-long study, the researcher interviewed teachers and students, took field notes, collected instructional planning documents, and photographed students' artifacts. Two questions guided the study:

1. How did the teachers use their knowledge and skills related to culturally responsive practices in an urban-multicultural classroom?
2. To what extent did they impact students in their overall learning process?

Theoretical Framework

This study is informed by Kroger's notion of identity theory (2007) and sociocultural theory (Vygotsky, 1978). These theories have informed my thinking about what it means for teachers to negotiate their identities as advocates for students and their communities. Thus, they affected how I observed, analyzed, and conceptualized their teaching and interactions. The core of identity theory is the categorization of the self as an occupant of a position, the incorporation into the self of the meanings and expectations associated with that position and its performance (Kroger, 2007). Therefore, self-knowledge is the foundation of who we are. Moreover, identity formation of teachers deepens the development of their own identity, culture, and how they interact with the curriculum in modeling their sense of belonging, which is needed to be effective in their classroom. Correspondingly, teachers with a positive identity will transfer that to students, especially the marginalized, who need it if they are to have the best educational experience.

Sociocultural theory suggests that learning occurs through social interaction and that social interactions are influenced by cultural and historical ways of knowing and doing (Vygotsky, 1978). Additionally, Banks (2019) and Sleeter (2013) contend that the dominant sociocultural knowledge of urban students is deficit oriented, and that knowledge has been solidified in the minds of teachers before they enter teacher education. Hence, critical sociocultural knowledge is a deeper form of sociocultural knowledge that can be drawn upon in flexible ways to act in educational spaces (Sleeter, 2013). This knowledge relates to the cultural and linguistic knowledge that students bring to the classroom, as well as their resources for interrogating and disrupting inequalities that are prevalent.

The Teachers' Identity-Oriented Approaches

Ms. Thomas and Mr. Jonathan

Ms. Thomas's background as a graduate of urban teaching fellows with a master's degree gave her the upper hand in connecting her social identities in professional identity development. Mr. Jonathan, as a co-teacher, had a similar background. As constructivists, both knew that their roles as educators were to facilitate students' unique needs and to see how knowledge and skills directly translate their success and families.

Further, they believed that dispositions matter in negotiating identity. During my first visit, I saw a class guided by firm expectations, deep commitment to students' success, and overwhelming enthusiasm. The teachers provided them with more than a lesson by showing care, reaching out to their families, and celebrating their successes. They worked with the after-school Senior College Prep group to meet their goal of timely graduations.

In addition, Ms. Thomas & Mr. Jonathan believed that self-knowledge brings depth to who they are and promotes greater understanding of others and their cultures. They expressed how they liked learning about their students' identities, whether they be cultural or ethnic, or their music tastes, tattoos, and friends, because these identities allowed them to make personal connections in order to push them academically.

Explication of teachers' identity-instructional orientation approaches

Data revealed that the two new teachers used three approaches: Equity Pedagogy (Banks, 2019; Sleeter, 2013); Cultural Competency (Gay, 2018; Villegas, 2007); and Academic Competency/Rigor (Dewey, 1964).

Equity Pedagogy. Equity pedagogy connotes using strategies to help students achieve fair and equal opportunities to learn (Banks, 2019; Sleeter, 2013). Both teachers used strategies to help students achieve fair and equal opportunities to learn. My classroom observation showed no preferential treatment of some or different students based on race, gender, immigration status, cultural and linguistic heritage, national identity, or creed. They created an environment wherein every student felt exceptionally safe and respected, and made appropriate and timely provisions for individual students. They brought multiple perspectives of examples in class and differentiated assessment methodologies. For example, during her lesson on Gothic writing and William Faulkner, Ms. Thomas began with students sharing their cultural stories, comparing them to the story William Faulkner wrote about the Southern Jim Crow era and rural life in the South. Then she paired them in twos, and they shared vocabulary, read relevant texts, and helped each other do the spelling test.

Similarly, Mr. Jonathan contended that acknowledging that all students have a story to tell helped him grow. He recognized how this made him more socially aware of the world around him, since classrooms are just a small world. At the same time, he believed that his identity kept on growing as he continued sharing his identity with them. For example, when he was working on the theme of the Holocaust and the Japanese internment camps during Week 10, he implemented equity pedagogy through team building, wherein students shared ideas both with one another and with teachers. He began class with this warm-up question: "Do you think there could ever be another Holocaust or Japanese internment camp? Why or why not?" Each student was asked to sit quietly and to individually answer these questions. Then, the two teachers went around checking how the students were doing. Next, he randomly divided them into small working groups. The groups discussed their answers and exchanged responses. Then each member shared his/her partner's response to the class.

Cultural Competency. This connotes displaying congruent attitudes, skills and behaviors of valuing diversity, ability to have cultural self-assessment, conscious of cultural dynamics in inter/intra-cultural situations, adaptability to diverse cultures and take initiatives of knowing surrounding cultures (Gay, 2018; Villegas, 2007). The two teachers loved and accepted other cultures by bringing cultural traits of students as a vehicle for learning. They were very adaptive to diverse cultures and took initiative to know about them. They incorporated culturally relevant literature in class with underlying statements of individual student cultural affirmation. They used culturally relevant assessment practices including assessments in students' native languages.

For example, when I observed Ms. Thomas in Week 7, I found the class to be highly interactive. She was teaching a unit based on differences between civil rights and human rights, and how humanity is fundamentally and morally bound to understand, implement, and advocate for others. Her knowledge of other cultures was systematically blended with robust examples from Korean imagery, Mexican symbolism, and Honduran music, which she displayed in class. The class resembled a showcase wherein all students spoke about how to take care of one another as a global society, with the motto of "unity in diversity." This majestic display was far-reaching for most immigrant students, who were learning for the first time what human and civil rights were, and how to be a part of the activism for oneself and for others. The most dramatic and interesting event of the lesson took place when one ELL-immigrant student, who never spoke any English, proudly volunteered to read his six-line poem about human rights in his Honduran native language to the class, and later discussed its meaning—line by line—in English. The poem expressed what it meant to be academically responsible to others, not only in class, but also any environment they found themselves in, because we are all members of the global family.

Evidently, Mr. Jonathan also challenged his own beliefs, values, and the cultural practices and structures surrounding his teachings. His instructional practices included active dialoguing, questioning, and building on responses from students' cultural inferences in order to deepen their understanding.

Further, his assignment and assessment practices were always authentic and situated, because he recognized the current problems and used them in practice.

Academic Competency/Rigor. This refers to the display of a great deal of content knowledge, enthusiasm, engaging in content and skills, having a complete acquisition of skills in the subject, and accomplishing this through challenging tasks and situated pedagogic styles (Dewey, 1964; Gay, 2018). Both teachers exhibited great enthusiasm when teaching and made the classes very exciting. At the same time, they displayed high expectations for meeting the standards and delivering clear objectives. In displaying rigor, they scaffolded the development of self-efficacy, personal identity, and agency in their instructions and interactions by exhibiting skills of working together in sharing and planning in a classroom (collegial planning). They continually shared the responsibilities of scaffolding students to meet their learning, emotional, and career goals.

In some instances, while Ms. Thomas took center stage providing instructions, Mr. Jonathan would move around the classroom assisting individuals and observing particular behaviors. I found this useful because students received individual help in a timely manner. For example, during a mid-November class, Ms. Thomas worked with students in understanding idiomatic language, onomatopoeia, and alliterations, thereby preparing them for a tough text that was the school district assignment. In the meantime, Mr. Jonathan was busy distributing papers for contextual examples and explorations. I observed Mr. Jonathan keeping students on-task when Ms. Thomas was in front or busy assisting others. He actually kept the class calm by watching over other students who might disrupt the flow of the class while emphasizing rigor.

How teachers used their knowledge and skills of culturally responsive practices in the classroom and communities for their development

Among many critical approaches, the teachers negotiated their identities by advocating for students and their communities. My year-long observation analysis conceptualized three aspects, namely: (a) Critical reflectiveness: that is, recognizing social, economic, and political inequities; (b) Problem-solving initiatives: that is, identifying problems and offering constructive solutions; and (c) Inquiry-based learning initiatives: that is, nurturing a spirit of inquiry through collaboration for the sake of establishing the validity of truth (Sleeter, 2013).

Critical Reflectiveness. The teachers were very authentic because they were able to criticize cultural norms, mores, and values, and to challenge mainstream knowledge. Ms. Thomas, for example, was critical of the school district and the curriculum. She contended that the district handed down the curriculum and pacing guide to the teachers and expected no modification. She also expressed that the curriculum, which was presented in a deficit model, was hurtful. Further, she acknowledged that the widely implemented testing syndrome strategy was detrimental, as it halted instructional innovations and caused anxiety and fatigue.

Mr. Jonathan, for his part, criticized Educational Preparation Programs (EPPs) for ignoring diversity courses and causing so many new educators to have limited knowledge about cultural diversity. For example, he said that he was aware of some EPPs that offered only one diversity course that lasted for a week, which he felt was not enough to foster in-depth knowledge to substantially support, culturally and linguistically, students of today's America.

Problem-solving initiatives. There are so many areas in which the teachers identified a problem and independently solved it. For example, they advocated the hiring of an additional social worker as compared to ten police offers in the building which was implemented. They contacted immigration attorneys, who enlightened students and families about their rights, citizenship responsibilities, and ways in which they could defend themselves. They contacted psychologists who visited the campus monthly to talk about psychological needs, including testing anxiety and the pressures of work in general. They provided technological support to students by soliciting used computers and brought in experts to help students with computer literacy. Finally, parents of many backgrounds were invited to visit the campus and talk about to their livelihoods, including their cultures and values.

Inquiry-based learning initiatives. The two teachers established a great collaborative co-teaching strategy that, they said, was a creative way to help students learn even more proficiently. They worked on a curricular development project, attended monthly professional development sessions, and engaged in action research projects in class to enhance their skills as new teachers. Through collaborative weekly lesson planning, they were made aware that some students are freer with one teacher over another, a fact that makes lessons interesting and more complete. Additionally, working as a team revealed individual talents and skills that they were able to use in community building of learners and ability levels.

Methodology

This research explores how the two teachers negotiated their identities as advocates for students in an Urban-Multicultural Classroom, despite the pressures of the prescriptive curriculum and mandated testing.

Study Context

This study took place during a full-year academic cycle in a large, urban-multicultural high school tenth-grade class that followed a traditional calendar. The school was within five miles of the downtown section of a large Midwestern city. The population of this school district was very urban, consisting mostly of low-income people, few of whom who resided in upscale apartments. The school served students from grades 7 to 12 and had an enrollment of 1,210. Of these students, 60% identified as Black, 20% identified as Hispanic, 13% identified as White, 4% identified as multiracial, and 3% identified as Asian. Among this group, 13% identified as English Language Learners (ELLs), with 71% participating in a free or reduced-price lunch program (Indiana State Department of Education, 2017).

For many years, this school has been trying to cope with typical urban problems such as pronounced lack of discipline, a high dropout rate, bullying, and very low academic performance, especially for students from cultural and linguistic minorities. According to the Indiana State Department of Education (2017), the school's overall performance grade was a low D. Only 37% of students from the school enrolled in college immediately after high school graduation, compared to the state average of 64%. In addition, 69% of graduates of this school required remediation, while the state average was 31%. It was a requirement for every student at the school to take a test after completing English 10. Students had to pass this state-required, end-of-course test to graduate from high school. In the 4 years before this study, as few as one out of ten students passed this test, and the pass rate was even worse for culturally and linguistically diverse students. The district administration tried to disrupt this pattern of failure by implementing a pacing guide, prescribed curriculum, and multiple practice tests, but these measures proved ineffective. At the beginning of the school year of this study, the school administration decided to try something new, a co-teaching arrangement for English Language Arts 10.

Data Collection

Data is one of the most important parts of this research study, because without compelling data I was cognizant of how difficult it could be to build a strong case. Using qualitative research methods, I looked at data with thick-descriptive paradigms as guidance, while at the same time aligning them with the research questions (Merriam, 2009). These data included curriculum documents like the resources, physical artifacts obtained from the school district, and the two participating teachers. They included lesson plans, progress grades, and teacher's journal reflections.

In addition, the researcher logged 15 classroom observations that included audio recordings and field notes. Further, I had seven in-depth, semi-structured open interviews with the two participating teachers, each of which lasted approximately 90 minutes. These were audio-recorded and transcribed within 24 hours.

Data Analysis

The bulk of the data analysis was conducted using the interactive model by Miles and Huberman (1994) and the research questions. Data analyzed from the original documents, transcribed audiotapes, interviews, and focus groups developed themes and coded. Miles and Huberman (1994) developed a comprehensive interactive model for analyzing data that helps the researcher to reflect and explore a visual reference on how data can be safeguarded, tracked, and tackled. These components were data collection, data reduction, data display, and verification and conclusion drawing. For example, following the components of the interactive model, the analysis of each collection of data followed the process of data reduction, data display, and verifying and drawing conclusions. The data reduction phase from the interviews and all other sources were simplified and organized into more easily manageable components over three phases. In the first phase, Level One, the interview was transcribed

(Merriam, 2009), and significant information was noted. Then each sentence or group of sentences was examined and given a label with a descriptive name.

Next, data were simplified further through the second phase (Level Two) coding process. In this stage, the Level One descriptive codes were merged into similar coded units to form categories, and these categories were given another pertinent label (Merriam, 2009; Miles & Huberman, 1994).

Miles and Huberman's data display embodies mapping out phase two and phase three categories on a chart in a simplified form. This chart displays how the categories are situated and indicates their relationship to each other (Merriam, 2009). Then, key themes were identified from each set of data set. Then I developed patterns and merged them. Finally, the researcher used NVivo (version 9) to organize and synthesize emerging themes.

Findings

In the following sections, I present key findings from data collected throughout the year. I organize findings by the following themes: growth of students in their construction of self and identity; growth in sociocultural consciousness; and overall academic growth.

Growth of students in their construction of self and identity

Over the course of the year, students evidenced tremendous growth in their self-esteem. They came to believe more in themselves, their dignity and worth, and looked toward their future with hope. They were more assertive, discovered their own beliefs and values, and saw their environment in new ways with new prospects. For example, during the last group interview, Jiman expressed the following sentiment, which echoed the impression for all of them:

> I feel like I have grown and I am different this time. I am a dynamic individual. I have changed in my thinking about life, I have grown in knowledge and I now know that I have power to contribute something in this class, this school, the community around and even beyond. I think I now know myself better than before. My classmates, my teachers, and the school community have made me grow and believe more in myself. I was shy at the beginning of this year and had very few friends, but now I have many friends and I feel happy.

Growth in sociocultural consciousness

Teachers negotiated their identities as advocates and facilitated students' awareness of other cultures. By using culturally appropriate practices and inclusive literature, students examined their own perspectives and reflected on their relationships and realized their role as active global citizens. The class became a community of learners. They developed empathy for one another and developed a social action awareness campaign to give back to the community. The climate and overall learning experiences led them not to fear diversity but to embrace it with dignity, confidence, and pride. Evidently, Nina expressed these sentiments during the interview:

> I like the classroom climate. Teachers are very friendly and helpful to me. I have grown not to fear diversity but approach it with pride, and I will advocate for others. I have learned more from my teachers who are calm, compassionate, and confident in their abilities in dealing with me, sharing these values through personal reflections and assignment and community building.

Academic Growth

As advocates, the new teachers' approach bore fruit in students' academic growth; indeed, it became evident virtually across the spectrum through improvement in grades. Students discovered the value of education and worked hard to achieve good grades. For example, Tim acknowledged that despite his struggles and disability status, he progressed well. He worked hard and wanted to do well. With his job and ambition to go for training in heating, ventilation, and air cooling (HVAC), he knew that he needed to work hard and obtain a high school diploma. From mid-semester on, he began attending tutoring twice a week in order to improve his grades. His progress report showed improvement. He had an F in September, C- in October, C+ in November, and B in December. His overall grade, including all submitted assignments, was B. This was the trend for everybody in class and was the fruit of hard work and resilience.

Discussion

From the findings, it is clear that what makes a good teacher is not only methodology or ideology, but also engagement with their identities and use of culturally responsive skills as advocates for students in an urban-multicultural classroom. The two teachers demonstrated their commitment to positive identity development, self-efficacy, and agency, despite the pressure of the prescriptive curriculum and mandated testing. Collaboration between them was beneficial, as they supported each other and students with cultural competency, academic efficacy, and sociocultural consciousness. As partners, they established and developed trust, open communication, respect, rapport, and problem-solving abilities with each other. Their dedication to teaching all students was evident, as they made it a priority to support them by incorporating culturally relevant learning resources and holding high expectations. They built a community of learners in class and even looked to the community beyond the classroom for support and connections. They used inquiry and critical reflectiveness to drive learning, and purposefully used inclusive strategies to create fair and equal opportunities to learn academic content.

Model for Culturally Competent Teacher Preparation Today

In the following section, I review what research has suggested are key components for Educator Preparation Programs (EPPs) that prepare new teachers today. (See Figure 1 below.)

Careful selection process: EPPs should begin with an early admission screening process that uses carefully constructed questions to reveal the dispositions of candidates. The program needs to find applicants who believe that all students can learn. The moral and ethical dimensions of teaching obligate teachers to teach all students fairly and with dignity and respect (Villegas, 2007). Moreover, history tells us that the U.S. educational system has favored one group while pushing the others to the margins, especially lower-income and racial/ethnic minority groups (Sleeter, 2013).

Improved Urban Education Program. Many scholars agree that EPPs comprise a disjointed body of theoretical curriculum for learning to teach, and also the pedagogy of teacher education (Sleeter, 2013). McDonald, Kazemi, and Kavanagh (2013) suggest that creating a common language and incorporating collective activity will help to improve the practice of new teachers and their identity. The program must unmask the assertion of color blindness, cultural conflict, myths of meritocracy, deficient thinking, and low expectations, which are prevalent prior to entering the program. In that way, EPPs can engage students in coursework with opportunities for teachers to develop skills, dispositions, and knowledge that unveil institutionalized and systemic practices—such as racism, sexism, classism, and discrimination—that exist in both the society and the classroom. The EPPs should focus on the pedagogy of formation of identity, self-efficacy, and sociocultural development, and the pedagogy of enactment in authentic settings and rigorous content knowledge.

Urban-based field experiences. EPPs must be the most viable vehicle for challenging dominant ideologies that allow students with traditionally marginalized social group membership, as well as those with dominant membership, to expand their understanding of reality (Apple, 2019). In order to bridge this gap, urban-based field experiences matter. Research has revealed that field experiences have served to build bridges between theory and practice for recent teacher graduates, who have become more effective in their practices (Sleeter, 2013).

Faculty mentoring and group support network. The fourth component of the module involves a comprehensive support network from faculty mentors. Recent literature has explored the correlation between being an effective urban teacher for the first 5 years and continued mentoring and professional support throughout (Sockett, 2009). This denotes the ongoing community affair where new teachers are assisted in reaching out to others to gain knowledge and experience of working with diverse students in theory and practice. Actually, mentoring helps them create ways of building critical conversations so that the actions followed lead to substantial progress based on goals that have been set.

Ideal teacher goal-set attributes. In all EPPs, candidates bring with them their personal, intellectual experiences from around the globe, their thoughts, and their feelings. However, in this model, the well-established goal-sets for fully prepared teachers are those well prepared as scholar professional, nurturer professional, clinician professional, and moral agent professional (Dewey, 1964; Sockett, 2009). As scholar professionals, they are robust in both pedagogical knowledge and pedagogical content knowledge. As nurturer professionals, teachers are prepared to care, nurture, and establish rapport with the vulnerable and disfranchised, especially multicultural-urban students and ELLs, and to know that their role is also to advocate for them (Villegas, 2007). As clinician professionals, teachers realize that teaching is a public good whose social purpose, among others, is to selfishly guard truths through collaborative research (Sockett, 2009). Finally, as moral agents, teachers are modelled to be defenders of moral integrity and to integrate academic and moral virtues in class in order to foster exemplary development and growth in kids as good citizens of the globe.

Learning never stops. Teachers are in a continuum. They value professional development, seminars, and collaborative inquiry to enrich themselves throughout their careers.

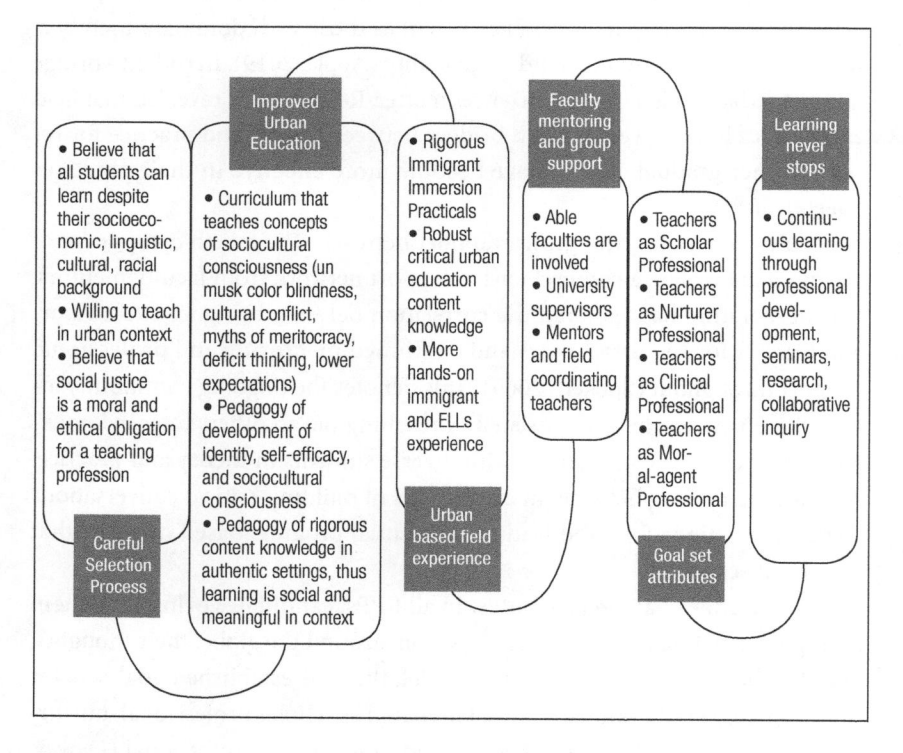

Figure 8.1.

Conclusion and Limitations

In this study I have focused on how teachers negotiate their identities as advocates for students who represent a diverse community. The study has demonstrated how the teachers use their sociocultural instructional skills to produce sufficient outcomes for at-risk students in an urban-multicultural Classroom. From a critical perspective, the teachers modified their curriculum and instructions, which were handed down by the school district by way of a deficient model, to create a more rigorous, student-centered approach in the constructivist model fitting today's multicultural, multilingual classrooms. The results were outstanding, with students demonstrating growth in their construction of self and identity, in their sociocultural skills, and in their academic growth.

Several limitations are important to note. This research was not designed to generalize all urban-multicultural students, or to compare them to all other minority groups. It was intended to provide a snapshot of these students, who were not only transformed emotionally, technologically, or in terms of their linguistic abilities, but who broadened their inner and outer concept of what it means to be successful today, despite challenges, through very strategic instruction skills.

However, further exploration is needed to determine whether the same could be true for other minority groups, or one specific immigrant group such as Asians or Africans in another location other than the Midwestern urban context in which this research was conducted. Finally, while this study has dealt with some immigrants and ELLs, the author did not specify their various immigrant statuses, such as refugee, HB-1 visa, and so forth. Therefore, any analysis of the impact of students' immigration status was not included in this study, even though such information might have provided insight into ways to improve outcomes for the at-risk students and reduce disparities in education systems.

References

Apple, M. (2019). *Ideology and curriculum* (4th ed.). Routledge.
Banks, J. (2019). *An introduction to multicultural education* (6th ed.). Pearson.
Danielewicz, J. (2014). *Teaching selves: Identity, pedagogy, and teacher education.* SUNY Press.
Dewey, J. (1964). The child and the curriculum. In R. D. Archambault (Ed.), *John Dewey on education: Selected writings.* University of Chicago Press.

Gay, G. (2018). *Culturally responsive teaching: Theory, research, & practice* (3rd ed.). Teachers College Press.

Indiana State Department of Education. (2017). *State K–12 School Data*. Retrieved from http://www.doe.in.gov/

Kroger, J. (2007). *Identity development: Adolescence through adulthood* (2nd ed.). Newbury Sage.

McDonald, M., Kazemi, E., & Kavanagh, S. (2013). Core practices and pedagogies of teacher education: A call for a common language and collective activity. *Journal of Teacher Education, 5*(1), 378–386.

Merriam, S. (2009). *Qualitative research: A guide to design and implementation*. Jossey-Bass.

Miles, M., & Huberman, A. (1994). *Qualitative data analysis: An expanded sourcebook* (2nd ed.). Sage.

Parten, B. (2016). Essential Civil War curriculum: The Port Royal experiment. *Virginia Center for Civil War Studies*. https://www.essentialcivilwarcurriculum.com/the-port-royal-experiment.html

Ryan, K., Cooper, J., & Bolick, C. (2019). *Those who can teach* (14th ed.). Cengage Learning.

Sleeter, C. (2013). *Power, teaching, and teacher education: Confronting injustice with critical action and research*. Peter Lang.

Sockett, H. (2009). Dispositions as virtues: The complexity of the construct. *Journal of Teacher Education, 60*, 291–303.

Villegas, R. (2007). Dispositions in teacher education: A look at social justice. *Journal of Teacher Education, 58*(5), 370–380.

Vygotsky, L. S. (1978). *Mind and society: The development of higher psychological processes*, ed. M. Cole, V. John-Steiner, S. Scribner, & E. Souberman. Harvard University Press.

NINE

Being Stuck: Autoethnographically En-gender-ing an Anti-sexist Teaching Praxis

Aaron Teo

Part 1: Dread

As I stand bolt upright at my desk in the staff room before the school day starts, I feel the dread in the pit of my stomach. It is thick and turbid, and I cannot rid myself of it. It has stuck to me, and I am stuck with it. I am dreading the upcoming meeting—a parent meeting in the middle of term three,[1] well after what is officially rostered;[2] a meeting which I had been summoned to out of the blue. The content of my teaching in my Year 12 Legal Studies class had become increasingly political over the school year and considering my precarious position as a part-time teacher in an unapologetically conservative high school, I anticipated that it was only a matter of time before I had to answer for my pedagogical decisions.

Unfortunately, beyond the gut feeling underlying this prediction, not much else was known. Perhaps it was the scholarship I had presented to the class debunking the myth of meritocracy (Young, 1958), or perhaps it was my overt anti-racist sentiments when it came to personal experiences with racism (Teo, 2021) and matters of legislative "protection" of Indigenous Australians (Jeffries & Bond, 2012; Snowball & Weatherburn, 2007). I speculated as well that it could have been my refusal to back down on the topic of race and gender privilege (McIntosh, 1988) and its relationship to leadership in Australian Parliament. Or maybe, it had to do with me linking all these intersections of disadvantage back to our school context. I wasn't sure which was the straw that broke the camel's back, and the deliberately vague correspondence from the parents only served to heighten my existing confusion and anxiety about the matter.

Following a volley of emails back and forth over the week, it was decided that we *needed* to speak in person, and so, here I was with laptop in hand and lump stuck in my throat. Rationally, I knew I had to start moving, lest I show up for the meeting late; emotionally, however, I remained stuck, completely rooted to the spot. Despite my best attempts to intellectualize[3] (Gabbard, 2010) which of the potential offenses I would be addressing, and ways in which I would then justify my pedagogical choices, I remain physically nauseous at the thought of the conversation that was to come. As I will myself away from the safety of my desk, I feel my heart hammer unevenly against my chest.

Part 2: Disapproval

There are just 15 minutes to go before the first lesson of the day, and as I usher Mr. and Mrs. S into the gaudy-colored classroom, I feel my head and the colors in the room swirling. Despite being in the middle of winter, I feel the beads of perspiration trickle down the small of my back. I pray that Mr. and Mrs. S haven't been able to sense my panic.

As I pull out the teacher's chair and steady myself, I notice an obdurate glint in Mrs. S's eye. We exchange pleasantries, and I slowly lower myself into the chair. I conduct a fleeting survey of the room, silently desperate for an excuse to excuse myself. There is none—I am stuck here with Mr. and Mrs. S. They have made themselves comfortable, so I brace myself for the impending onslaught.

"Right, we know that you need to teach soon, so we might jump straight in. This has to do with the email you showed to Lawrence and the other students that day."

I take a moment to process this and realize that my initial conjectures were close—alas, it was the deputy principal's email to a close female colleague that had set all this in motion. This was no ordinary email, though. It was an emphatically condescending reply to the concerns my colleague raised about the unnecessary density of staff bodies on campus during the recent government-mandated COVID-19 lockdown (Queensland Health, 2021). It was also a prime example of workplace bullying, and an artifact that I had shown to my ostensibly mature Year 12 students as part of a Human Rights unit in a bid to call out internalized misogyny and sexism in the workplace.

"Now, we wanted to speak to you because we just don't think that what you did was appropriate."

Being Stuck 135

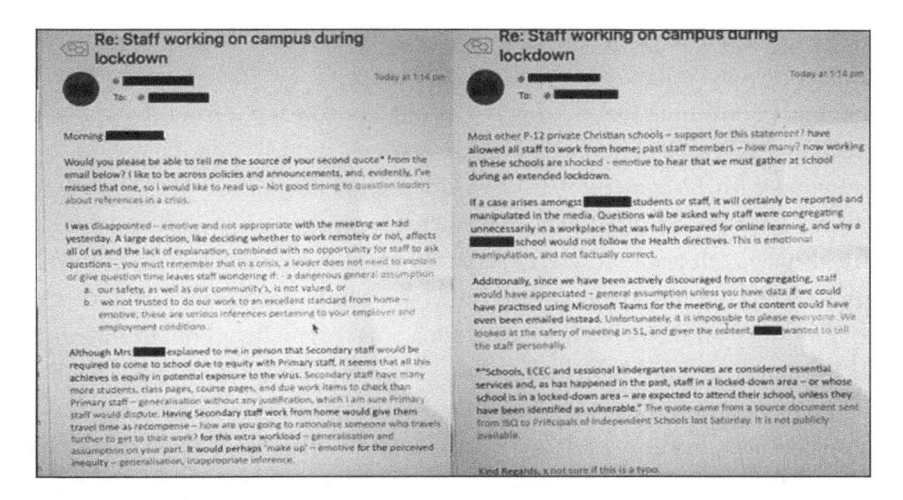

Figure 9.1. The email shown to my Year 12 Legal Studies students.

Note: The red text is the deputy principal's response to the original email in black and blue text. In Queensland, P–12 refers to Prep to Year 12—that is, Prep is the first year of schooling (age 5), all the way up to Year 12 (age 17 or 18), the final year of schooling. S1 was the on-campus room in which staff were instructed to meet. ECEC stands for Early Childhood Education and Care, while ISQ is short for Independent Schools Queensland, the state-wide peak body for independent schools. From A. Teo (personal communication, August 16, 2021).

Mr. S interrupts Mrs. S with an awkward laugh and finishes her sentence with the fact that Lawrence has always been a huge fan of my classes and that they just wanted to give me a chance to explain what I did.

My internal dialogue is screeching at a thousand decibels, but I somehow manage to sputter the following in response.

"Well, in line with our current Human Rights unit, my main motivation was to highlight how common it is for women to face different forms of discrimination in the workplace. Because this email was from a female school leader to a female teacher, it was also a good example of internalized misogyny on the sender's part—an instance of fulfilling the values of the dominant, patriarchal society while not accounting for the implications that her approach would have on the lives of other women (Ruddick, 1980).[4] Importantly, it demonstrated that sexism can be perpetuated by *both* men and women (Prasad et al., 2020), which, in my opinion, has very real implications for everyone in class."

Mrs. S looks quizzically at me, while Mr. S quickly regales me with a quick tale about his previous experience as a teacher.

"So yes, I sort of get where you're coming from, Aaron, but having been a teacher myself, I'm aware of just how much influence I've had on my students, and I just don't think that sharing something like this sets a good example or sends the right type of message."

I ponder Mr. S's contention briefly before responding.

"Yes, I completely agree with what you're saying about influence, and this is *exactly* why I felt it was crucial to show the email to the students. All of them are stepping out into the real-world next year, and I don't want *any* of them to have to be on the receiving end of such a nasty email and not know why it's happened, or worse still, end up being someone who *sends* such an email."

"Particularly for the boys, it's no longer enough for them to not be perpetrators of such forms of violence against women—they need to be speaking up against it, too, lest they end up *perpetuating* the situation (Flood & Ertel, 2020). My contention was that comfortably distancing themselves from outright perpetrators did not necessarily make them any more innocent, and that a preference for an individualized and depoliticized approach (Göransson, 2014) to questions of sexual discrimination was deeply harmful. After all, 'a great many men who draw [on what scholarship refers to as] the patriarchal dividend also respect their wives and mothers, are never violent towards women, do their accustomed share of the housework, bring home the family wage, [but at the same time] can easily convince themselves that [anything to do with feminism and gender equality must involve] bra-burning extremis[m]' (Connell, 2005, p. 80)."

"Now, I probably *could* have opted for a depersonalized account of sexism and workplace bullying from the textbook or the Internet, but as a researcher, I believe there is a personal-political-pedagogical impetus (Mackinlay, 2019) to share this. In doing so, I certainly *hope* that students are influenced by it— influenced to speak out and work against such behavior if, and when, the time comes! I've been telling them from the start of the year that when it comes to inequity, there is a moral obligation to bother by *being* bothered (Ahmed, 2014). Fundamentally, the email was deidentified, and the recipient encouraged me to share the information, so I believe it made for a germane teaching opportunity."

There is a momentary lull following my justification wherein I feel slightly more courageous. However, Mr. S's dropped jaw and Mrs. S's raised eyebrows tell me that it hasn't been particularly well-received. The ensuing silence in the room is deafening. Eventually, Mrs. S responds.

"Hmm, while we can *appreciate* where you're coming from, Aaron, we still don't think it was suitable to share in class. I mean, sure, if it was an example from the past, that wouldn't have been *as* bad, but the fact that it's ongoing and *in this school*... I'm sorry to say this, but you've put Lawrence in a *very* difficult and uncomfortable position, particularly in his role as Student President. You know, he came home after your class that day and was quite distressed about all of this. Surely, you could have spoken to someone *else* about all of this instead of involving the students?"

I reel back when I hear this—I am somewhat disconcerted by the rebuke but am caught completely off-guard by the distinct lack of active listening and empathy. All I can muster in response at that moment is a sheepish smile, which seems to function as a cue for Mr. S to weigh in with *his* disapproval.

"Yes, students are *highly* impressionable, and I think all showing them the email did was model how to disrespect authority. I don't think that's something we can agree with, so we would appreciate if you could do something about this. We would really *prefer* not to bring this matter to upper management, which is why we've spoken to you first. We hope you understand where *we're* coming from."

My internal dialogue screams in anguish, and I feel the lump stuck in my throat engorge. Why could they not see that foremost in this situation was an "equality problematic" (Lodge & Lynch, 2004, p. 139) for both teachers and students due to the inherent power relations in the school? Why was it so "difficult to accept that [this situation had come about in the first place precisely because such] institutions are substantively, not just metaphorically, gendered" (Connell, 2005, p. 73) and gendering locations (Keddie, 2021)?

I am stuck for what to say, so I take a deep breath and force a smile for Mr. and Mrs. S.

"I see. What *would* you like me to do?"

Part 3: Disappointment

It is the day after my meeting with Mr. and Mrs. S. As I stand at my desk in the staffroom yet again—this time with head lowered and back hunched—I find myself thrown out of my usual routine, unable to focus on the simple administrative task in front of me. Having taken the previous evening to emotionally unpack how the meeting unfolded, I am stuck with a bitter, lingering sense of what could only be described as disappointment. You see, having shaped my teaching across the year around the intent of "making visible the relationships among knowledge, authority and power" (Giroux, 2010, p. 336), I was certain that I had done enough to "challenge students to critically engage with the world so they can act on it" (Giroux, 2010, p. 336)—certain that I had capitalized on the various opportunities available to disrupt gender inequality in school (Gowlett & Niesche, 2017). Indeed, despite Lawrence's largely imperialist, sexist, and racist (hooks, 2015) worldview at the start of the course, I was reasonably certain that most of my "pedagogical risk-taking" (Breunig, 2016, p. 5) had gotten through. Either way, I had resolved to no longer engage in an "act of complicity" (hooks, 1994, p. 66) by remaining silent about such matters. I was cognizant that my "talking about sexism and racism [was] heard as damaging institutions," yet I knew that my teaching praxis had to embody a commitment to damage institutions (Ahmed, 2017). To that end, showing the students the condescending email was meant to be the *coup de grace* in the year-long battle against their deeply entrenched privilege. For Lawrence in particular, it was a matter of calling out his "unearned privilege associated with being a man in a culture that is inherently phallogocentric" (Prasad et al., 2020, p. 1579), a privilege that manifested in a self-sustaining discourse of entitlement that reifies male domination of the classroom (Keddie, 2009).

How wrong I was, of course! As I stand at my desk, still with head lowered and back hunched, I imagine the myriad ways in which Lawrence's conversation with Mr. and Mrs. S might have unfolded. That his first instinct was to complain to his parents should not have surprised me. It was, after all, indicative that "classrooms are not homogenous environments with a common understanding of oppression, but deeply divided places where contested narratives are steeped in the politics of emotion to create complex emotional and intellectual challenges for teachers" (Zembylas, 2013, p. 181). I should have realized that this typical reactionary response (Flood, 2019) was characteristic of the fact that questions of feminism, equality, and equity "automatically bring up…negative overtones and pushback from boys" (Keddie, 2021, p. 179), since ingrained patriarchal constructions of masculinity make it difficult for men like Mr. S and Lawrence to move beyond a "narrowly construed objectivity" (Hopkins, 1998, p. 43) to embrace alternative perspectives toward violence and gender (John Kall & Roberts, 2010). Alas, I should also have been cognizant that male privilege so deeply structures men's identities, opportunities, and moment-to-moment interactions, that men's embrace of the full extent that privilege has shaped their lives would be destabilizing to the point of immobility (Kahane, 1998). Indeed, the deep discomfort that Lawrence felt from my calling out sexism in a highly familiar school context that systematically privileges boys/men (Connell, 2000) and subsequent challenge to avoid an "ongoing complicity in patriarchal privilege" (Flood, 2014, p. 43) was likely commensurate with a "loss of personality structure that may [have] been quite terrifying; a kind of gender vertigo" (Connell, 2005, p. 137).

I slowly take a seat and try to rationalize this, but instead remain stuck with "feelings of anger . . . and disappointment with men" (hooks, 2014, p. 192), and Lawrence in particular.

Part 4: Doubt

A couple of weeks have passed since the meeting with Mr. and Mrs. S. Some of the anger has subsided, but the disappointment lingers.

As I continue to teach the Year 12 Legal Studies class, I realize that I am stuck yet again.

Here I was, doing the work of a "tempered radical" (Meyerson & Tompkins-Stange, 2007, p. 311) and seemingly embodying a form of "ally politics" (Flood, 2019)—but to what effect? Despite what I thought were my best efforts at disrupting the discourses of masculinity that spoke Lawrence into existence (Davies, 1997), I had failed, and we were clearly back at square one.

Even more significantly, I realize that my "speaking and writing about [gender inequality] raises complex practical-theoretical-political-ethical concerns, haunted by the specter of . . . engaging in yet another imposition" (Prasad et al., 2020, p. 1589). I hear Braidotti's (1994) chastisement that:

> What the heterosexual men are lacking intellectually—the peculiar blindness to sexual difference for which the term sexism is an inadequate assessment—is a reflection of their position in history. They have not inherited a world of oppression and exclusion based on their sexed corporal being; they do not have the lived experience of oppression because of their sex. Thus, most of them fail to grasp the specificity of feminism in terms of its articulation of theory and practice, of thought and life. (p. 138)

Indeed, Kahane (1998) corroborates that as a man, involvement with feminism is an oxymoron, leaving me with a deep uneasiness that in talking about gender inequality, I "involuntarily appropriate the term which does not belong to me and to which I am not entitled" (Prasad et al., 2020, p. 1592). Knowing as well that "privilege [is] indelibly inscribed onto men, and men embody it whether they choose to or not" (Kimmel, 1998, p. 62), I cannot shake the question of whether, as a heterosexual man from a middle-class background, I can truly resist the patriarchy (Rosenberg, 2017). From this position of privilege, I am mindful that by exploring the positions of those less privileged, there is the danger of my privileged assumptions causing me to unknowingly misrepresent the other's story (Young, 1997), and so, I wonder how I can possibly "do representation knowing that I can never quite get it right" (Pillow, 2003, p. 176)—a conundrum of being stuck in "gender limbo" (Ekelund, 2020).

At the same time, as a heterosexual man who is also a racial minority in the overwhelmingly white Australian educational landscape (Sleeter, 2001), I have been disempowered due to my race and ethnicity (Kimmel, 1998; Teo, 2021), and, as a result of my experiences with difference and marginalization as well as the "relational interests" (Mills, 2013) involving the aforementioned incident with my close female colleague, I desire to disrupt and speak back to the hierarchical and exclusionary understandings of gender at play (Martino & Pallotta-Chiarolli, 2003) as an ethical imperative (Kimmel, 1998). I am aware that making my position transparent doesn't make it unproblematic (Spivak, 1988) and so continue to press along with a "degree of lived, articulated ambivalence" (Prasad et al., 2020, p. 1589).

To some extent, I am comforted by hooks's (2014) assurance that "a male who has divested of male privilege, who has embraced feminist politics, is a worthy comrade in struggle, in no way a threat to feminism" (p. 12), and Connell's (2000) encouragement that supporting women's emancipation is certainly a possible posture for men. Mills (2013) further argues that it is problematic to propose that "men cannot engage with feminism in supportive ways ... [since it] suggest[s] that it is not possible for *anyone* [emphasis added] who benefits from a current system of oppression to act in ways that potentially undermine that privilege" (p. 200). Crucially, because "feminism provides both women *and* [emphasis added] men with an extraordinarily powerful analytic prism through which to understand their lives, and a political and moral imperative to transform the unequal conditions of those relationships" (Kimmel,

1998, pp. 60–61), there is an indisputable urgency for us men to persist with a clear, socially just, feminist focus that challenges the patriarchy (hooks, 2014).

Back at my desk following a Legal Studies lesson closer to the end of term three, I am distracted from a menial administrative task yet again as I start to wa/onder about "'what to do next' in academic work [and praxis] that hopes to be of use in struggles for social justice" (Lather, 1998, p. 488); about how to proceed after being ambivalently stuck back at square one with Lawrence. I am reminded of Patti Lather's (1998) "praxis of stuck places," which disrupts the "right story" (p. 487) of what effective pedagogy should look like—a praxis instead of constant movement, of never finishing, closing, or defining, and of not being sure, which situates "the experience of impossibility as an enabling site" for working through doubt, and appreciates the "between space of any knowing that will make a difference in the expansion in social justice and the canons of value toward which we aspire" (p. 495). I wa/onder if perhaps being stuck with/in this ambivalence is a way to account for the "necessary misfirings of pedagogy" (Lather & Ellsworth, 1996, p. 1) and the "practices of confounding disruptions" (Pillow, 2003, p. 192) that sit "within 'the impossibility of teaching" in order to "produce and learn from ruptures, failures, breaks, and refusals" (Lather, 1998, p. 495).

Indeed, the failure that was Lawrence's refusal is a germane lesson and reminder of the continued importance of rupturing and renouncing membership in the club of masculinity and risking fears of rejection when confronting other men (Kimmel, 1998) as a way of challenging "any sense of entitlement they might feel in relation to their privilege and to provide them with opportunities to resist that privilege actively" (Mills & Keddie, 2007, p. 350). Of course, such challenges necessitate learning from, and remaining accountable to, women, to ensure critical self-reflection and political legitimacy (Luyt & Starck, 2020)—a way of remaining "vigilant about our practices" (Spivak, 1984, p. 184) as men. This learning is an ongoing, lifelong process (Burrell & Flood, 2019), steeped in a posture of humility that simultaneously recognizes that male involvement is central to changing gendered cultures and practices when boys/men positively influence the views and behavior of other boys/men (Messner et al., 2015), but also unsettles our "self-assurance in what we know" (Sellar, 2012, p. 61)—a process that recognizes that men are "necessary, but not sufficient elements" (Kimmel, 1998, p. 68) in the fight for gender equality. Perhaps being stuck in this liminal space means that we can avoid the dangers of "white knight politics" (Mills, 2013), being "hypervisible" (Messner et al., 2015), or wholly reshaping the movement's interests around ourselves (Hopkins, 1998)—a space where we can acknowledge men's experience without privileging it (Kimmel, 1998), since it is "not men's place to make claims about which direction the women's movement should take" (Burrell & Flood 2019, p. 239).

Perhaps being stuck means that I can seek to know while situating that very knowing as tenuous (Pillow, 2003) as I work through similar pedagogical "examples that may not always be successful, examples that do not seek a comfortable, transcendent end-point but leave us in the uncomfortable realities of doing" the work (Pillow, 2003, p. 193); a continuous effort that doesn't fold or "take refuge in the futility of self-critique . . . [but rather is] as aware as possible of its inevitable shortcomings" (Lather, 1993, p. 685). In willing to be stuck, I am hopeful of the possibilities it affords for thinking and acting against the gendered grain by "connecting critical learning to the experiences and histories that students bring to the classroom, and engaging the space of schooling as a site of contestation, resistance and possibility" (Giroux 2003, p. 6).

Perhaps being stuck with/in this ambivalence might involve a whole lot of "questions, freedom and unease" (Greene, 2001, p. 166), which is fine, especially if it prevents me from "speaking too loudly, too frequently, or with assumed author-ity" (Prasad et al., 2020, p. 1591). Perhaps being stuck means that I am always "in quest" (Greene, 2001, p. 159) and "always on the way" (Greene, 1994, p. 217) in shaping a "practice to a future that must remain to come" (Lather, 1998, p. 497).

Notes

1. Out of a four-term school year.
2. At this school, parent-teacher meetings usually take place at the beginning of terms one and three.
3. A defense mechanism that uses reasoning to delay/avoid confrontation with an internal conflict and its associated stressors.
4. hooks (2014) refers to this internalized sexism as "the enemy within," resulting in sexist thinking that causes women to "judge each other without compassion and punish one another harshly" (p. 14). This stems from being "in a culture of domination [where] everyone is socialized to see violence as an acceptable means of social control" and where "dominant parties [like the deputy principal] maintain power

by the threat (acted upon or not) that abusive punishment, physical or psychological, will be used whenever the hierarchal structures in place are threatened" (p. 64).

References

Ahmed, S. (2014). *Willful subjects*. Duke University Press.
Ahmed, S. (2017, October 24). Institutional as usual. *feministkilljoys*. https://feministkilljoys.com/2017/10/24/institutional-as-usual/
Braidotti, R. (1994). *Nomadic subjects: Embodiment and sexual difference in contemporary feminist theory*. Columbia University Press.
Breunig, M. (2016). Critical and social justice pedagogies in practice. In M. Breunig & M. A. Peters, (Eds.), *Encyclopaedia of educational philosophy and theory*. Springer.
Burrell, S., & Flood, M. (2019). Which feminism? Dilemmas in profeminist men's praxis to end violence against women. *Global Social Welfare, 6*(4), 231–244.
Connell, R. (2000). *The men and the boys*. Allen & Unwin.
Connell, R. (2005). *Masculinities* (2nd ed.). Allen & Unwin.
Davies, B. (1997). Constructing and deconstructing masculinities through critical literacy. *Gender & Education, 9*(1), 9–31.
Ekelund, R. (2020). Young feminist men finding their way. On young Swedish men's experiences of and orientations in feminist settings. *Culture Unbound, 12*(3), 506–526.
Flood, M. (2014). Men's anti-violence activism and the construction of gender-equitable masculinities. In A. Carabi & J. Armengol (Eds.), *Alternative masculinities for a changing world* (pp. 35–50). Palgrave Macmillan.
Flood, M. (2019). *Engaging men and boys in violence prevention*. Palgrave Macmillan.
Flood, M., & Ertel, D. (2020). Concluding critical commentary: Men's experiences as agents of feminist change. In R. Luyt & K. Starck (Eds.), *Masculine power and gender equality: Men as change agents* (pp. 181–199). Springer.
Gabbard, G. (2010). *Long-term psychodynamic therapy: A basic text* (3rd ed.). American Psychiatric Association Publishing.
Giroux, H. (2003). Public pedagogy and the politics of resistance: Notes on a critical theory of educational struggle. *Educational Philosophy and Theory, 35*(1), 5–16.
Giroux, H. (2010). Paulo Freire and the crisis of the political. *Power and Education, 2*(3), 335–340.
Göransson, C. (2014). *Rejecting violence, reclaiming men: How men's work against men's violence challenges and reinforces the gender order*. Stockholm University.
Gowlett, C., & Niesche, R. (2017). Learner diversity and school practices. In B. Gobby & R. Walker (Eds.), *Powers of curriculum: Sociological perspectives on education* (pp. 353–371). Oxford University Press.
Greene, M. (1994). Postmodernism and the crisis of representation. *English Education, 26*(4), 206–219.
Greene, M. (2001). *Variations on a blue guitar*. Teachers College Press.
hooks, b. (1994). *Teaching to transgress: Education as the practice of freedom*. Routledge.

hooks, b. (2014). *Ain't I a woman: Black women and feminism*. Taylor and Francis.
hooks, b. (2015). *Feminism is for everybody: Passionate politics* (2nd ed.). Routledge.
Hopkins, P. D. (1998). How feminism made a man out of me: The proper subject of feminism and the problem of men. In T. Digby (Ed.), *Men doing feminism* (pp. 33–56). Routledge.
Jeffries, S., & Bond, C. E. W. (2012). The impact of Indigenous status on adult sentencing: A review of the statistical research literature from the United States, Canada, and Australia. *Journal of Ethnicity in Criminal Justice, 10*(3), 223–243.
John Kall, B., & Roberts, B. (2010). Exploring the involvement of men in genderbased violence prevention programmes in settings affected by armed conflict. *Diversity and Equality in Health and Care, 7*(3).
Kahane, D. J. (1998). Male feminism as oxymoron. In T. Digby (Ed.), *Men doing feminism* (pp. 213–236). Routledge.
Keddie, A. (2009). "Some of those girls can be real drama queens: Issues of gender, sexual harassment and school." *Sex Education, 9*(1), 1–16.
Keddie, A. (2021). Engaging boys in issues of gender activism: Issues of discomfort and emotion. *Gender and Education, 33*(2), 171–185.
Kimmel, M. S. (1998). Who's afraid of men doing feminism? In T. Digby (Ed.), *Men doing feminism* (pp. 57–68). Routledge.
Lather, P. (1993). Fertile obsession: Validity after poststructuralism. *Sociological Quarterly, 34*(4), 673–693.
Lather, P. (1998). Critical pedagogy and its complicities: A praxis of stuck places. *Educational Theory, 48*(4), 487–497.
Lather, P., & Ellsworth, E. (1996). Introduction: Situated pedagogies. *Theory into Practice, 35*(20), 1.
Lodge, A., & Lynch, K. (2004). *Equality and power in schools: Redistribution, recognition and representation*. Routledge.
Luyt, R., & Starck, K. (2020). Only for the brave? Political men and masculinities: Change agents for gender equality. In R. Luyt & K. Starck (Eds.), *Masculine power and gender equality: Masculinities as change agents* (pp. 1–14). Springer.
Mackinlay, E. (2019). *Critical writing for embodied approaches*. Springer.
Martino, W., & Pallotta-Chiarolli, M. (2003). *So what's a boy?* Open University Press.
McIntosh, P. (1988). *White privilege and male privilege: A personal account of coming to see correspondences through work in women's studies*. ERIC Clearinghouse.
Messner, M., Greenberg, M., & Peretz, T. (2015). *Some men: Feminist allies in the movement to end violence against women*. Oxford University Press.
Meyerson, D. E., & Tompkins-Stange, M. (2007). Tempered radicals as institutional change agents: The case of advancing gender equity at the University of Michigan. *Harvard Women's Law Journal, 30*(2), 303–322.
Mills, M. (2013). Men, feminism and education: Personal reflections. In M. B. Weaver-Hightower & C. Skelton (Eds.), *Leaders in gender and education: Intellectual self-portraits* (pp. 193–204). Brill Sense Publishers.

Mills, M., & Keddie, A. (2007). Teaching boys and gender justice. *International Journal of Inclusive Education, 11*(3), 335–354.

Prasad, A., Centeno, A., Rhodes, C., Nisar, M. A., Taylor, S., Tienari, J., & Alakavuklar, O. N. (2020). What are men's roles and responsibilities in the feminist project for gender egalitarianism? *Gender, Work, and Organization, 28*(4), 1579–1599.

Pillow, W. (2003). Confession, catharsis, or cure? Rethinking the uses of reflexivity as methodological power in qualitative research. *International Journal of Qualitative Studies in Education, 16*(2), 175–196.

Queensland Health. (2021, August 2). *Queensland COVID-19 update* [press release]. https://www.health.qld.gov.au/news-events/doh-media-releases/releases/queensland-covid-19-update13

Rosenberg, I. (2017). *"A lifetime of activism": Doing feminist men's work from a social justice paradigm*. Master's Thesis, University of Victoria. UVicSpace. https://dspace.library.uvic.ca/handle/1828/8636

Ruddick, S. (1980). Maternal thinking. *Feminist Studies, 6*(2), 342–367.

Sellar, S. (2012). "It's all about relationships": Hesitation, friendship and pedagogical assemblage. *Discourse: Studies in the Cultural Politics of Education, 33*(1), 61–74.

Sleeter, C. E. (2001). Preparing teachers for culturally diverse schools: Research and the overwhelming presence of Whiteness. *Journal of Teacher Education, 52*(2), 94–106.

Snowball, L., & Weatherburn, D. (2007). Does racial bias in sentencing contribute to Indigenous overrepresentation in prison? *Australian & New Zealand Journal of Criminology, 40*(3), 272–290.

Spivak, G. C. (1984). Criticism, feminism and the institution. *Thesis Eleven, 10*(11), 175–189.

Spivak, G. C. (1988). Can the subaltern speak? In C. Nelson & L. Grossberg (Eds.), *Marxism and the interpretation of culture* (pp. 271–313). University of Illinois Press.

Teo, A. (2021). A timed crisis: Australian education, migrant Asian teachers and critical autoethnography. In H. Kara & S-m. Khoo (Eds.), *Qualitative and digital research in times of crisis: Methods, reflexivity and ethics* (pp. 191–203). Policy Press.

Young, I. M. (1997). *Intersecting voices: Dilemmas of gender, political philosophy, and policy*. Princeton University Press.

Young, M. (1958) *The rise of the meritocracy, 1870–2033: An essay on education and equality*. Thames & Hudson.

Zembylas, M. (2013). Critical pedagogy and emotion: Working through "troubled knowledge" in posttraumatic contexts. *Critical Studies in Education, 54*(2), 176–189.

TEN

Critical Disability Studies as Methodologies for Social Change: The Use of Participatory Research Methodologies in Social Research with Women and Girls with Disabilities in the Global South

Xuan Thuy Nguyen, Tammy Bernasky, Marnina Gonick, and Claudia Mitchell

Conceptualizing Critical Disability Studies as Methodology

In "Enabling whom: Critical Disability now," Julie Avril Minich (2016) offers a vantage point for rethinking the epistemic foundations of disability studies. According to Minich (2016), disability studies should be recognized as a methodology rather than an object of study. This approach could tackle the tension between research about disabled people and research that, despite not immediately being recognized as disability studies, has the potential to investigate normative systems of power, privilege, and oppression. In other words, the methodology of disability studies emphasizes ways of scrutinizing the social norms that produce categories of difference "with the goal of producing knowledge in support of justice for people with stigmatized bodies and minds" (Minich, 2016, para 6).

Sami Schalk (2017) observes that Minich's methodology of disability studies enables us to engage with the ways in which ability and disability are mutually constituted within a system of social norms that categorizes and (de)values certain bodyminds. Schalk (2017) uses the parenthetical designation of *(dis)ability* to refer to the mutually dependent nature of disability and ability, emphasizing "how the boundaries between disability and ability are uneven, contestable, and context dependent" (para. 3). Interestingly, however, while both Minich (2016) and Schalk (2017) highlight the need to see disability in relation to race and other intersectional categories within the historical context of the United States, they both leave untouched the discursive and material production of disability in transnational contexts.

There is a silence on the materiality of disability in contexts of the global South, where experiences of disability, gender, race, and ethnicity may be vastly different from those in the North (Soldatic & Grech, 2016; Mehrotra, 2020). Scholars from the global South point to the complex consequences of colonialism and Western imperialism in the embodied experiences of disabled people in distinctive Southern contexts (Meekosha & Soldatic, 2011; Puar, 2017; Mehrotra, 2020; Figueroa & Hernández-Saca, 2021). And yet, as Grech (2015) observes, disability studies in the global North have disengaged with writings on disability outside of Northern contexts, where voices and epistemologies from the South are usually pushed to the peripheries (see also Goodley & Swartz, 2016). It is thus useful to ask: What might the methodology of disability studies do in colonial and imperialist contexts, where diverse voices of disabled people have been largely silenced by the global North? What methods and methodologies can be used to shed light on the systems of power that produce ableism, disablism, racism, classism, and male patriarchy in Southern contexts?

Emerging from the work of decolonial scholars (Mignolo & Walsh, 2018) and disability scholars in colonized spaces in Indigenous and Southern contexts (Figueroa & Hernández-Saca, 2021), the field of decolonial disability studies offers a methodology for understanding theories and methods from historically colonized spaces. This collective body of knowledge, research, and praxis works to unsettle Western regimes of knowledge by unveiling the "coloniality of power" (Quijano, 2000) in relation to its production of marginalized bodies and minds. Recognizing difference as a part of humanity that one depends on in the process of world-making, decolonial disability studies reclaims the existence of and relationship with bodies, minds, spirits, and hearts that have been historically seen as sick, disabled, and, as such, uncivilized. Instead, they re-engage with struggles of marginalized voices and communities from the South as a form of world-making and resurgence that creates transformation from within (Mignolo & Walsh, 2018).

Literature Review

The majority of people with disabilities live in the global South, and more than half of them are women and girls (Dowse et al., 2016) who experience marginalization and exclusion within education, work, economic activities, family life (Price & Goyal, 2016), and access to justice (Dowse et al., 2016; United Nations Population Fund, 2018). Even so, there is a significant gap in research that centers the experiences of women and girls with disabilities within their specific contexts. Specifically, while international human rights frameworks include people with disabilities, women and girls with disabilities in the South are underrepresented in theory and in practice (Mehrotra, 2013; Nguyen, 2016; Nguyen et al., 2019; Soldatic & Samararatne, 2020). In fact, most research and writing about disability experienced in the global South comes from interventions made by researchers in and from the North (Swartz, 2018). This is concerning because girls and women with disabilities from the global South are subject to additional barriers, including colonial and imperialist violence (Erevelles, 2011, 2014; Puar, 2017; Nguyen, 2019). They also experience discrimination based on their religion, caste, ethnicity, gender, and other aspects of identity (Ghai, 2002, 2015; Connell, 2011; Mehrotra, 2020; Shah & Bradbury-Jones, 2018).

As a signatory to the Convention on the Rights of Persons with Disabilities, Vietnam has developed policies and laws that protect people with disabilities from discrimination, such as the Law on Persons with Disabilities (Socialist Republic of Vietnam, 2010). Still, there are challenges around its legal constructions and implementation. This law renders Vietnamese women and girls with disabilities invisible. Women and girls with disabilities are more likely to experience barriers accessing education than those without disabilities. Socioeconomic status, rural location, as well as gender, disability, age, and ethnicity discrimination affect girls with disabilities and their access to education in Vietnam (Nguyen et al., 2015; United Nations, n.d.). Furthermore, girls with disabilities in Vietnam are situated within a specific neo-liberal context of rapid socio-economic reform seen with Vietnam's Doi Moi policy, decentralization and privatization of services, and ongoing practices of state control and population surveillance (Stienstra & Nguyen, 2020). Thus, despite its rights-based discourse, the law fails to address the ongoing exclusion and marginalization of women and girls with disabilities within a neoliberal condition that views the root causes of disability as located within the individual instead of society.

The uncritical transfer and application of disability rights originally produced in the global North to Southern contexts risks creating problematic universalizations of disability when, in fact, people's lived experiences are shaped and formed within their local contexts. This universal construction of disability is based on a historical assumption that there are commonly held beliefs and homogenous interpretations of disability that can be applied to any context without properly considering the socio-political conditions and impact of local beliefs or practices. These neo-colonial ideologies of disability have come from the global North and are deeply rooted in colonial legacies (Rao & Kalyanpur, 2020). Critical disability studies that emerge in the global South recognize that the majority of the world's population has been colonized and rejects this oversimplification of disability (Elder & Migliarini, 2020).

A critical disability studies informed by a decolonial approach ensures that research with and by people with disabilities is participatory and context-driven (Elder & Migliarini, 2020). Drawing on, and learning from, disability theories and praxis from the global South as a critical place of knowledge production, we can engage with this knowledge through centering perspectives and experiences of women and girls with disabilities from the global South (Nguyen, 2016, 2019). This begins the process of recognizing the value that women and girls with disabilities and their communities bring to movements while drawing on their collective agency as a foundation for social justice in the global South.

Case Study: The TDKRA Project

Transforming Disability Knowledge, Research, and Activism (TDKRA) is a research project funded by the Social Sciences and Humanities Research Council of Canada (2016–2020). The project aims to tackle the cultural and historical absence of girls with disabilities in the global South by engaging disabled girls in Vietnam in developing their knowledge and building potential for collective activism. While the TDKRA project did not start with a decolonial disability studies approach, it sets the stage for the development of decolonial disability studies by seeking to unsettle the boundaries between research and activism that are framed within Western academic institutions and to rebuild research relations with communities in the Global South (Nguyen et al., 2019). In TDKRA, we use an interdisciplinary, community-engaged, decolonial and participatory arts-based approach. We also apply an intersectional lens to explore complex categories of "disability" and encourage a more nuanced understanding of differences within intersectional categories of disability, gender, ethnicity, age, and region. This approach sheds light on the ways in which these aspects of identity intersect and shape individual experiences. At the same time, these experiences occur within contexts and structures that impact experiences of oppression and privilege within Southern spaces.

Our decolonial approach is developed throughout a research process where our team works to create inclusive and decolonial spaces for knowledge production: building relationships between the research team and Disabled People's Organizations (DPOs) in Vietnam; training women with disabilities through mentorship with girls with disabilities; using participatory visual research with girls with disabilities to raise their perspectives and tackle their exclusion; and fostering community-engaged relationships to mobilize knowledge across local, trans-local, and transnational communities (Nguyen, 2020). We engage in participatory research with women and girls with disabilities in three disadvantaged communities in Vietnam: Bắc Từ Liêm (an urban district in Hà Nội, in northern Vietnam), A Lưới (a rural district in the central province of Thừa Thiên Huế), and Bình Thuỷ and Ninh Kiều (urban districts in the southern province of Cần Thơ). These communities are distinct in terms of their socio-economic, ethnic, and political locations in Vietnam. In total, we engaged with 86 women and girls with disabilities (55 girls and 31 women). The girls (between the ages of ten and twenty-one) were the knowledge producers, while the women (between the ages of twenty and forty-eight) were co-facilitators and mentors to the girls. The majority of our participants came from poor, working-class, and in the case of participants in A Luoi, ethnic minority status.

Methodology

The use of Participatory Visual Methodologies (PVM) in TDKRA's three research sites in Vietnam builds on, but also *refines*, an extensive body of work with marginalized participants and communities that is based on visual tools and approaches such as drawing, photovoice, digital storytelling, and participatory video/cellphilming. The naming of this assemblage of participatory approaches known as PVM is relatively recent (see Gubrium & Harper,

2013; Mitchell et al., 2017), and draws on rich traditions of visual studies (see Mitchell, 2011; Rose, 2012). This work also continues to evolve as we see with studies, often visual, that explicitly refer to research with youth (Youth Participatory Action Research or YPAR). The specific approaches to PVM date back to the late 1980s and early 1990s, building on the strengths of participatory research, the critical frameworks of feminist studies, and more recently the social studies of childhood and youth studies that recognizes the strength of participant-led methodologies in seeking to amplify their voices on issues that are of concern to them.

Of significance to critical disability studies is that these approaches, which have always sought to be inclusive and democratizing (Mitchell, 2011), go a step further by adopting a stance that seeks to be decolonial. Specifically, who is producing the drawings of inclusion/exclusion? Who is behind the camera or manipulating the cellphone or tablet? When we add "where?" to the equation, these approaches used in the global South also serve to engage non-Western decolonial knowledge production (Nguyen, 2020). In previous publications we have described some of the methodological considerations of using the various PVMs in our work with girls and women with disabilities: photovoice (Nguyen et al., 2015), drawing (Nguyen, 2020), and cellphilming (Nguyen et al., 2021), along with addressing key ethical issues (Mitchell et al., 2016).

Drawing: As Theron et al. (2017) note, drawing as a research methodology typically involves some version of draw-write-talk, with participants having the opportunity to create oral or written captions to go with their drawing, with the possibility for also narrating a story or participating in a semi-structured interview. For group settings we also add in on-site exhibitions, which give participants the opportunity to engage with and respond to the collection of drawings. The display mode can be a very simple clothesline and can be accompanied by small group discussions organized around several questions (see Nguyen et al., 2021).

Cellphilming: The use of cellphones to create cellphilms, or short videos, is a PVM that builds on a youth-friendly tool (cellphones) based on relatively widespread access to mobile technology (see MacEntee et al., 2016). The process of participatory video and cellphilming as mapped out elsewhere (Mitchell & De Lange, 2019) involves a number of steps based on small groups working with a specific prompt or question: brainstorming, reviewing filming techniques and logistical concerns such as sound, creating a storyboard or

Critical Disability Studies as Methodologies for Social Change

plan, filming, small-group reflection, whole-group screening, and discussion. As argued elsewhere, the use of an everyday technology that is already part of the repertoire of many of the participants is in and of itself a decolonial approach to storytelling (Nguyen et al., 2021).

In the first workshop with participants in A Luoi, we organized a 2-day event with participants. In the workshop, participants were given an option to draw or create objects with clay materials. The activity lasted for 30–40 minutes. The participants were invited to tell us about their creations. We also asked participants to comment on the relevance of their creations to their own lives. In what follows, we address key findings of this workshop. We will also present findings from the cellphilm workshops with girls with disabilities in all three communities.

Findings

Disability, livelihoods, and survival: Stories from the global South

While we recognized a relationship between disability, livelihood, and survival for women and girls with disabilities in all communities, we found this concern most poignant in A Luoi. The findings suggest that women and girls with disabilities in A Luoi experienced much more poverty and exclusion than in other communities. In their conversations, the participants talked about their struggles with poor health conditions, lack of access to healthcare services, and exclusion from schools. Most participants, especially the women, expressed a desperate need to sustain family livelihoods, wanting to have a house, a piece of land to grow their crops, or a chance to raise cattle and chickens. All women expressed a need for job opportunities. A woman shared that "Farming is not enough for us to save money" and therefore "I cannot afford to buy water and food." Another woman said that "My mother has been in the hospital. I am living with my sister who is suffering from heart disease. Life is hard. My family cannot afford to pay for the cost of living." In telling their own stories, participants were also sharing stories about their family members and communities.

The drawings reflect their struggles for survival. Our analysis triangulated the drawings, their discussions, and the narratives generated in different workshops to make sense of the productions. Figure 1 was produced by a 14-year-old girl with visual impairment whom we refer to as Thuong.[1]

Figure 10.1. Artwork produced by Thuong, Age 14, A Luoi, 2017.

Thuong draws a rural space with a banana tree, a range of mountains, and a glimpse of sunshine in the background. At the center is a woman standing by a house with two chickens on her right. At the bottom of the picture is a farmer who appears to be harvesting in the field. There is another field coloured in blue with some trees across the field. Phuong described her drawing: "My drawing is about my parents. My father is working and my mother stays at home. My mother is not able to work because of her hand pain."

While the drawing appears to convey a sense of livelihoods within a traditional kinship system with ethnic minority origins, the story also reflects the relationship between disability and the lack of livelihoods in the lives of these young women. For instance, Phuong told us that her mother could not work because of the pain in her body but did not indicate its cause. This story resonates with those of many women with disabilities who expressed their struggles with illness and poverty, and yet their desire to live a productive life.

Production was drawn by Hong and shows how ethnic minority women with disabilities are working to sustain their lives. The image shows a woman pouring grain to feed two little chicks. Her house is surrounded by a field of growing crops in the top left corner. In the bottom right, she draws another

Figure 10.2. Artwork produced by Hong, Age 32, A Luoi, 2017.

field, some plants, and a pond beside it. There is a tree, along with a dome-like haystack. As Hong describes it, "The topic of my painting is Production. I hope my family will have a garden to provide food, grow vegetables, raise chickens and fish."

It appears that Hong is drawing her hope to sustain her family's livelihood. In her discussion, she shared that her dream had not come true, so this is more about desire than reality. Hong shared that she experienced significant hardship with family illnesses and hospitalizations. With very limited family resources, Hong found herself in a very difficult situation. She also faced multiple layers of discrimination due to her ethnicity and disability. The story below was told by Hong in a workshop when the girls and women reflected upon their own lived experience of discrimination.

> There was one time when I went to the hospital guest-house to rest. One person asked me: "Are you from ethnic minority group?" I replied, "Yes. I am from an ethnic minority group," and then she said," people from ethnic minority groups are dumb." I just asked her: "Why did you say I am dumb?" She said, "Because you are a member of an ethnic minority group." I asked, "Auntie, do you know

how to speak an ethnic language?" She said: "No." I said: "So why did you say, you are dumb because you do not know the ethnic minority languages." She had no words to say. I was so angry because they said people from ethnic minority groups are stupid.

This story reflects multiple layers of oppression that ethnic women and girls with disabilities face in communities in the global South. In contrast, the drawings reflect their collective desire for living in their local spaces beyond mere survival.

Re-Storying Disability through Cellphilm-Making

The use of cellphilming in the TDKRA project offered girls with disabilities an opportunity to re-story their experiences. In contrast to the Western framing of girls with disabilities as absent and vulnerable bodies, their recollections tell more complex stories about disability and intersectional identities. One poignant theme identified through the productions is their common experiences with discrimination, as demonstrated in *Paying a Price, Don't Look Down on Children with Disabilities, A Dream of a Girl with Disabilities, Rising Up,* and *Please Respect Us!* Through these productions, the girls explored their treatment by their able-bodied peers.

A cellphilm produced in A Luoi, titled *Rising Up*, shows this dynamic. The film begins with a disabled girl walking upstairs toward her classroom. Her disability is depicted through her difficult climb, and yet the physical experience with stairs calls into question the inaccessible space that renders her movement difficult. More poignantly, the film shows the discriminatory attitude of her peers. A group of friends stands on one side of the stairs laughing loudly and violently pointing at her. One classmate abruptly runs over and shoves her to the ground. The girl stands up and continues into the classroom. The disabled girl is silenced.

The next scene shows a group of students sitting in a classroom. A teacher (played by a disabled woman) is assigning tasks to her students. One girl stands up, points at the disabled girl, and shouts: "You are a disabled person. You are not allowed to join this group to study with us. Get out of class. We do not want to be infected by your disease." Other classmates applaud. This time, instead of remaining silent, the disabled girl responds: "Disability is not an infection. Don't treat me like that." In the last scene, the group shows a message about their film: "Do not look at our impairment. Please look at our capacities!" In their discussion, they add that "(non-disabled) people shouldn't despise people with disabilities!" The disabled girl's character shifted from being a victim of bullying to one who powerfully intervenes into able-bodied norms. Her statement that "disability is not an infection" and "Don't treat me like that!" calls out the ableism shaping school exclusions.

In *Equality Rights*, a group of girls in Bac Tu Liem tell a similar narrative about disability discrimination, but it involves complex relationships with family and community members. This cellphilm demonstrates that the girls are conscious of the discriminatory attitudes of non-disabled parents. The film begins with some girls playing together. The mother of a non-disabled girl orders her non-disabled child to "Go home! Why do you play with those disabled girls?" The disabled girls show signs of sadness. In the second scene, a shift in the film narrative is depicted with the non-disabled girl falling on the floor while running. We see the girls with disabilities coming over to help her. It ends with the mother recognizing that she treated the girls badly and apologizes.

In brainstorming this story, the disabled girls tell their own stories about being "abused," "hit," and "cursed." When asked what subject she wants to communicate through her film, Lém Linh said: "Maybe it is about school. I want to resist the bullies." When asked if she had some experience with abuse, she said that she was called "cripple," but then "I fought back. . . . I was going to hit them." Other times, she describes "bending down, covering your ears" to resist the violence. Clearly, the imaginative process of creating the film narrative and the discussion during the film-making process enabled the girls to express their own experience with disabilities and how they are treated by able-bodied people.

Through their film narratives, the participants reveal multiple layers of oppression. In the two films *Gender* and *Paying a Price*, gendered relations are revealed through the differential treatment of boys and girls in the family (*Gender*) and through forms of violence performed by boys in schools (*Paying a Price*) (Nguyen et al., 2021). In *Paying a Price*, the participants demonstrate their awareness of how gender discrimination plays out in school. The following excerpt shows an exchange among the girls and a woman with disabilities, who facilitates their discussion, about how to frame the narrative of their film:

Mickey: ... Introduce the title of the film first, then explain the "paying a price"!

Facilitator: that's right, we introduce and explain the title of the film "Paying a Price." Diem, tell us what pay a price means?

Diem: Because the boy teases the girl, so he has to pay a price for that.

Facilitator: But why is the girl teased? What's the issue with the girl?

Diem: She is a disabled person.

Facilitator: You have to say that the boy himself is the person . . . what?

Diem: The boy is the person who pays a price for the teasing.

Facilitator: Ok. That's right, so you have to tell them [the audience] that the boy in this film is the person who has to pay, but why?

Diem: Because he teases the girl with disability.

Facilitator: That's right, how does the boy pay?

Diem: Go to the girl and say sorry.

Unlike *Rising Up*, where the girl's embodied experience with disability is highlighted as central to the story, *Paying a Price* highlights the everyday experience in schooling where gender intersects with disability oppression to shape disabled girls' experiences. The girls offer a solution for tackling this patriarchal relationship by having the boy apologize to the girl.

In these productions, participants take control over their narratives. Questions regarding control of narratives is extremely important in the context where disabled girls in the global South are usually represented in Western discourses as simply vulnerable bodies. What the disabled girls chose to represent, instead, are their collective stories. The use of pronouns such as "we" and "ours" instead of "I" or "my" in their discussion suggests that these stories represent a part of their common experiences with schooling. The cellphilms also highlight actions proposed by the girls, suggesting their capacities to use cellphilming as a method for picturing their experience and demanding change.

Discussion

PVM shares many of the emancipatory and decolonizing goals of feminist, participatory action and youth resistance methodologies. Each is concerned with how research can be a tool for working toward social justice for marginalized communities and for changing the ways in which these communities are represented and discussed within academic research. Moreover, at the center of these methodologies is an active role for research participants to engage in their own knowledge-making practices, one that counters how marginalized communities are often understood as damaged, passive, and unable to be the creators of knowledge.

In her examination of the symbolic violence of the academy, bell hooks (1990) critiques the ways these communities are commonly treated in academic research:

> No need to hear your voice when I can talk about you better than you can speak for yourself. No need to hear your voice. Only tell me about your pain. (p. 343)

For Guishard and Tuck (2014), this is a colonial form of research, appropriating others' experiences for professional gain and locating power outside of communities. In contrast, in its use of PVM, the TDKRA project is invested in creating pathways for the voices of women and girls living with disabilities in the global South to be heard and for them to speak for themselves through the production of their artwork. PVM is a method in which girls and women with disabilities living in the global South are engaged as experts in their own lives, as complex people whose lives consist of more than just pain, as co-theorists, and as having perspectives worth sharing. However, despite the de-colonizing aspirations of PVM, there are still many ethical, political, and epistemological dilemmas that need to be engaged when doing this kind of research.

PVM can take many forms, and what any such project might look like will depend on a range of factors, such as the goals of the research, the experience of the researchers and participants, the access to materials, the context of the research, and the funding (Mitchell, 2011). The availability of new and relatively inexpensive technologies such as cell phones, video cameras, and disposable cameras has contributed to the increased interest in this way of working with young people. Many of the Vietnamese girls did not have access to cell phones, and so the making of the cellphilms was a technological novelty. This methodological approach is decolonial in that it challenges Western hegemony of knowledge production where theory, methods, and technologies are exported from the global North to the global South, with little understanding of the local contexts. In fact, as we observed in our fieldwork, some of the young women were very adept at using computers and social media (more so than the researchers). One woman worked on adding sound and visual effects and making other edits to the cellphilms.

Our decolonial approach shifts the focus of theory and practice to people with lived experience as a way of resisting the hegemony of Western theory and epistemologies. We focused on researching *with* women and girls with disabilities in their own communities about things that mattered to them in their daily lives. The disruption of Northern-driven research agendas through context-specific, participant-driven research processes challenges the risk of universalization of disability that has underscored much of disability studies discourse. Instead, our research methods advance transnational disability studies through knowledge production with and within the global South.

Part of the decolonizing efforts of PVM, like other participatory methodologies, is to try to shift the dynamic between researchers and researched, from one where research is conducted *on* or *about* to one where research is *with* participants. With the use of researcher-generated prompts, TDKRA participants shaped the content, form, and approaches taken in the art they produced. They were involved in decisions about display of the work and how to present it to the local officials invited to the final days of each workshop. In this way, a certain reciprocity emerges in the relationships between researchers and researched. Researchers are not merely going into a community and extracting the information or data they need for their own purposes, and participants also gain something beyond the skills that may be learned or the intrinsic pleasure of creating art with others. Sometimes what is gained is framed as empowerment, voice, and/or agency. However, as Gonick (2017) suggests, even with this shift in the research dynamic, it is important not to romanticize relations between researchers and researched. As feminist researchers have argued for decades, there are always unequal power relations shaped by differences such as age, race, gender, class, disability, and sexuality, and these need to be engaged with, acknowledged, and theorized by researchers (Alcoff, 1995; Behar & Gordon, 1995). One strategy for resisting and undoing colonizing reiterations of authorial and epistemic privilege, advocated by Maggie McClure (2013), is what she calls moments of productive disconcertation. Drawing on postcolonial feminist writing (Mohanty, 1988; Visweswaran, 1994), she argues that embracing interpretive hesitancy as an orientation to research and data analysis can be framed as a decolonising methodological logic that disrupts the reproduction of comfortable and normative master narratives that center adult, White, middle-class western, heterosexual, cisgendered, and able-bodied forms of knowing.

PVM not only allows for the expression of the girls' subjugated knowledge and re-orients adult-child conversations to focus less on adult assumptions, preconceptions, and concerns, and more on those of young people. It also offers the opportunity to imagine alternatives to what currently exists. As de Leeuw and Rydin (2007) suggest, arts practice offers young people the possibility of placing themselves in imaginative cultural identities, what one could be, even if just for a moment. This is particularly useful for disability studies, as it offers a way of re-imagining disability within decolonial spaces. In the cellphilms, the disabled girls present alternative ways of understanding what it means to live with a disability and to demand better treatment, relationships, and supports from their families, friends, communities, and society at large. As Wendy Luttrell (2010) writes, arts projects open up opportunities to unsettle, fragment, or dislodge other's gazes, where young people can see themselves and be seen by others in alternative ways to those that have framed them and the communities they come from—for example, as creative, thoughtful, engaged, and articulate. This opportunity to "theorize back" (Tuck, 2008) has the potential to shift the language/narrative of theory and policy so that they do not speak against the interests of girls and women living with disabilities in the global South.

Conclusion

Our aim has been to deepen an understanding of how arts-based, community-engaged, decolonial and participatory research can be used to engage girls and women with disabilities in the global South. In showing this work "in action" through our case study with girls and women with disabilities in three sites in Vietnam, we have sought to offer a more conceptually nuanced framework for arts-based participatory research both "in" and "as" critical disabilities studies. On the one hand, our argument, which rests on compelling evidence from the drawings and the cellphilms of girls and women with disabilities, suggests that participatory visual methodologies would more broadly benefit from a decolonial "turn" in order to account for shifts in power and control, as well as how stories are told and interpreted. On the other hand, and for the purposes of this article, we are advocating for a re-framing of this work within the context of our research with girls and women with disabilities as an entry point to mapping out critical disability studies as methodologies for social change. In order to do this, we have highlighted several key themes, including re-assessing the alignment between the media for engagement (e.g., digital media) and the themes and terms of engagement proposed by the participants themselves, and as exemplified even in the titles of their productions (*Equality Rights, Rising Up*). We regard this framing of what we term "critical disabilities studies as social change" as providing a much-needed platform for incorporating the work of Tuck, Connell, and other scholars into this methodological space.[2] This approach creates a decolonial turn that speaks to Minich's and Schalk's critical disability studies as methodologies from the perspectives of women and girls with disabilities in the global South.

Discussion questions

1. What are some key challenges of Western disability studies in relation to research with disabled people in the global South?
2. What does it mean to shift disability studies from an object of inquiry to methodology?
3. In what ways can Participatory Visual Methodologies be decolonizing?
4. How can drawing and cellphilm-making be used as a participatory tool for re-storying disability?
5. How can decolonial PVM be used for social change within disability studies and beyond?

Activities

1. In groups of 3–4 students, create a 3-minute cellphilm on a topic that you find most pertinent to disabled people and their communities. Use the following steps in creating a cellphilm: brainstorming, creating a storyboard, filming, small-group reflection, whole-group screening, and discussion. Do not worry if you have never created a short cellphilm before. This is a learning process. See an example of the cellphilming process and any examples of cellphilms at https://internationalcellphilmfestival.com/

2. Reflecting on your cellphilming process and product, how can this approach empower disabled people to re-create their own narratives? How can this approach be decolonial, especially for those in historically colonized spaces?

Notes

1. We use the participants' nicknames in this chapter to protect their identities.

2. Several decades ago, Schratz and Walker (1995) proposed the then-radical notion of "research as social change." This has been followed by various iterations and adaptations, including "visual methodologies for social change" (DeLange, et al., 2007), "research as intervention" (D'Amico et al., 2016), and, of course, the broad category of participatory visual methodologies as well as Youth and Participatory Action Research (YPAR), often incorporating the visual and other arts-based approaches. While there is certainly overlap between and among these terms, just as "critical disabilities studies as social change" will have some overlap, there is for each a biography that supports the coining of a specific term.

References

Alcoff, L. (1995). The problem of speaking for others. In J. Roof & R. Wiegman (Eds.), *Who can speak? Authority and cultural identity* (pp. 97–119). University of Illinois Press.

Behar, R., & Gordon, D. A. (Eds). (1995). *Women writing culture*. University of California Press.

Connell, R. (2011). Southern bodies and disability: Re-thinking concepts. *Third World Quarterly, 32*(8), 1369–1381.

D'Amico, M., Denov, M., Khan, F., Linds, W., & Akesson, A. (2016). Research as intervention? Exploring the health and well-being of children and youth facing global adversity through participatory visual methods. *Journal of Global Health, 11*(5–6), 528–545. doi: 10.1080/1744 1692.2016.1165719

De Lange, N., Mitchell, C., & Stuart, J. (Eds.). (2007). *Putting people in the picture: Visual methodologies for social change*. Sense.

de Leeuw, S., & Rydin, I. (2007). Migrant children's digital stories: Identity formation and self-representation through media production. *European Journal of Cultural Studies, 10*(4), 447–464.

Dowse, L., Frohmader, C., & Didi, A. (2016). Violence against disabled women in the global South: Working locally, acting globally. In S. Grech & K. Soldatic (Eds.), *Disability in the Global South, International Perspectives on Social Policy, Administration, and Practice* (pp. 323–336). Springer International Publishing.

Elder, B., & Migliarini, V. (2020). Decolonizing inclusive education: A collection of practical inclusive CDS-and DisCrit-informed teaching practices implemented in the global South. *Disability and the Global South, 7*(1), 1852–1872.

Erevelles, N. (2011). *Disability and difference in global contexts: Enabling a transformative body politic*. Palgrave Macmillan.

Erevelles, N. (2014). Crippin' Jim Crow: Disability, dis-location, and the school-to-prison pipeline. In L. Ben-Moshe, C. Chapman, & A. C. Carey (Eds.), *Disability incarcerated: Imprisonment and disability in the United States and Canada* (pp. 81–99). Palgrave Macmillan.

Figueroa, C., & Hernández-Saca, D. I. (Eds.). (2021). *Dis/ability in the Americas: The intersections of education, power, and identity*. Palgrave Macmillan.

Ghai, A. (2002). Disabled women: An excluded agenda of Indian feminism. *Hypatia, 17*(3), 49–66.

Ghai, A. (2015). *Rethinking disability in India*. Routledge.

Gonick, M. (2017). About us by us and other stories of arts-based research and marginalized girls. In X. Chen, R. Raby, & P. Albanese (Eds.), *Sociology of Childhood and Youth in Canada* (pp. 89–105). Canadian Scholars Press.

Goodley, D., & Swartz, L. (2016). The place of disability. In S. Grech & K. Soldatic (Eds.), *Disability in the global South* (pp. 69–83). Springer.

Grech, S. (2015). *Disability and poverty in the global South: Renegotiating development in Guatemala*. Palgrave Macmillan.

Gubrium A., & Harper, K. (2013). *Participatory visual and digital methodologies*. Left Coast Press.

Guishard, M., & Tuck, E. (2014). Youth resistance research methods and ethical challenges. In E. Tuck & K. W. Yang (Eds.), *Youth resistance research and theories of change* (pp. 181–194). Routledge.

hooks, b. (1990). Marginality as a site of resistance. In R. Ferguson et al. (Eds.), *Out there: Marginalization and contemporary cultures* (pp. 241–243). MIT Press.

Luttrell, W. (2010). A Camera is a big responsibility: A lens for analysing children's visual voices. *Visual Studies, 25*(3), 224–237.

MacEntee, K., Burkholder, C., & Schwab-Cartas, J. (Eds.). *What's a cellphilm? Integrating mobile phone technology into participatory visual research and activism*. Sense.

McClure, M. (2013). The wonder of data. *Cultural Studies—Critical Methodologies, 13*(4), 228–232.

Meekosha, H., & Soldatic, K. (2011). Human rights and the Global South: The case of disability. *Third World Quarterly, 32*(8), 1383–1397.

Mehrotra, N. (2013). *Disability, gender & state policy*. RAWAT publications.

Mehrotra, N. (Ed.) (2020). *Disability studies in India: Interdisciplinary perspectives*. Springer.

Mignolo, W., & Walsh, C. (2018). *On decoloniality: Concepts, analytics, praxis*. Duke University Press.

Minich, J. A. (2016). Enabling whom? Critical disability studies now. *Lateral, 5*(1).

Mitchell, C. (2011). *Doing visual research*. Sage.

Mitchell, C., & De Lange, N. (2019). Community-based participatory video and social action. In L. Pauwels & D. Mannay. *Sage handbook of visual research methods* (2nd ed.) (pp. 254–266). Sage.

Mitchell, C., De Lange, N., & Moletsane, R. (2017). *Participatory visual methodologies: Social change, community and policy*. Sage.

Mitchell, C., De Lange, N., & Nguyen, X. T. (2016). The participation of girls with disabilities in Vietnam in a photovoice project. In J. Coffey, S. Budgeon, & H. Cahill (Eds.), *Learning bodies—The body in youth and childhood studies*. Springer.

Mohanty, C. (1988). Under western eyes: feminist scholarship and colonial discourse. *Feminist Review, 30*(1), 61–88.

Nguyen, X. T. (2016). Girls with disabilities in the global South: Rethinking the politics of engagement. *Girlhood Studies: An Interdisciplinary Journal, 9*, 53–71.

Nguyen, X. T. (2019). Unsettling "inclusion" in the global South: A post-colonial and intersectional approach to disability, gender, and education. In M. J. Schuelk, C. Johnstone, G. Thomas, & A. Artiles (Eds.), *The SAGE handbook of inclusion and diversity in education* (pp. 28–40). SAGE.

Nguyen, X. T. (2020). Whose research is it? Reflection on participatory research with women and girls with disabilities in the global South. *Jeunesse: Young People, Texts, Cultures, 12*(2), 129–153.

Nguyen, X. T., Dang, T. L., & Mitchell, C. (2021). How can girls with disabilities become activists in their own lives? Creating opportunities for policy dialogue through "knowledge mobilisation spaces." *Agenda*, 1–13.

Nguyen, X. T., Gonick, M., & Bui, T. (2021). Engaging girls with disabilities through cellphilming: Reflections on participatory visual research as a means of countering violence in the Global South. *Childhood, 28*(3), 380–394.

Nguyen, X. T., Mitchell, C., De Lange, N., & Fritsch, K. (2015). Engaging girls with disabilities in Vietnam: Making their voices count. *Disability and Society, 30*(5), 773–787.

Nguyen, X. T., Stienstra, D., Gonick, M., Do, H., & Huynh, N. (2019). Unsettling research versus activism: How might critical disability studies disrupt traditional research boundaries? *Disability & Society, 34*(7–8), 1042–1061.

Price, J., and Goyal, N. (2016). The fluid connections and uncertain spaces of women with disabilities: Making links across and beyond the global South. In S. Grech & K. Soldatic (Eds.), *Disability in the Global South, International Perspectives on Social Policy, Administration, and Practice* (pp. 303–322). Springer International Publishing.

Puar, J. K. (2017). *The right to maim: Debility, Capacity, Disability*. Duke University Press.

Quijano, A. (2000). The coloniality of power and Eurocentrism in Latin America. *International Sociology, 15*(2), 215–232.

Rao, S., & Kalyanpur, M. (2020). Universal notions of development and disability: Towards whose imagined vision. *Disability and the Global South, 7*(1), 1830–1851.

Rose, G. (2012). *Visual methodologies: An introduction to researching with visual materials* (3rd ed.). Sage.

Schalk, S. (2017). Critical disability studies as methodology. *Lateral, 6*(1). Retrieved from http://csalateral.org/issue/6-1/forum-alt-humanities-critical-disability-studies-methodology-schalk/

Schratz, M., & Walker, R. (1995). *Research as social change: New opportunities for qualitative research*. Routledge.

Shah, S., & Bradbury-Jones, C. (2018). *Disability, gender and violence over the life course: Global perspectives and human rights approaches*. Routledge.

Socialist Republic of Vietnam (SRV). (2010). *Law on Persons with Disabilities (51/2010/Qh12)*. Labour and Society Publishers.

Soldatic, K., & Grech, S. (Eds.). (2016). *Disability and colonialism: (Dis)encounters and anxious intersectionalities*. Routledge

Soldatic, K., & Samararatne, D. (2020). *Women with disabilities as agents of peace, change and rights: Experiences from Sri Lanka*. Routledge.

Stienstra, D., & Nguyen, X. T. (2020). Opening to the possible: Girls and women with disabilities engaging in Vietnam. In S. M. Wiebe & L. Levac (Eds.), *Creating spaces for engagement* (pp. 139–160). University of Toronto Press.

Swartz, L. (2018). Representing disability and development in the global south. *Medical Humanities, 44*(4), 281–284.

Theron, L. C., & Mitchell, C. (2017). Drawing is only for kids, right? Wrong—Drawing as participatory visual methodology. In K. Tomaselli (Ed.), *Making sense of research: Theory, practice and relevance* (pp. 231–238). Van Schaik.

Tuck, E. (2008). Theorizing back: An approach to participatory policy analysis. In *Theory and Educational Research* (pp. 121–140). Routledge.

United Nations. (n.d.). *Women with disabilities fact sheet*. Retrieved from https://www.un.org/development/desa/disabilities/resources/women-with-disabilities-factsheet.html

United Nations Population Fund. (2018). *Women and young persons with disabilities: Guidelines for providing rights-based and gender-responsive services to address gender-based violence and sexual and reproductive health and rights*. United Nations Population Fund & Women Enabled International. https://www.unfpa.org/featured-publication/women-and-young-persons-disabilities

Visweswaran, K. (1994). *Fictions of feminist ethnography*. University of Minnesota Press.

About the Authors

Benedict Adams, Ph.D., a graduate of Indiana University is the Assistant Professor of the Department of Education at Missouri Western State University, St. Joseph, MO. Dr. Adams is the author of eight peer reviewed research articles including a book chapter. A prolific author and an academic scholar, Dr. Adams research interests are on Teacher Education and Culturally Responsiveness, Teacher development and socialization, and Historical & Social Foundations of Education. Dr. Adams can be reached at badams16@missouriwestern.edu.

Tammy Bernasky is an Assistant Professor in Political Science in the Department of L'nu, Political, and Social Studies at Cape Breton University. She holds a PhD in Critical Disability Studies from York University and specializes in gender and disability-based violence. Using an intersectional lens, Tammy centers the stories of people with disabilities in her teaching and research.

Fatima Brunson, PhD. is post-doctoral researcher in the School of Education at the University of Pittsburgh. Dr. Brunson earned her doctorate degree in Policy Studies in Urban Education from the University of Illinois at Chicago (UIC). Her research is used to connect literature on workplace conditions, teachers collaborative practice and culturally responsive and sustaining pedagogies.

Tanja Burkhard is a qualitative researcher and Assistant Professor of Human Development at Washington State University. Her work centers the development of critical, feminist, and anticolonial qualitative research methodologies that lend themselves to explorations of racialization, (im)migration, gender and language in education.

Pat Lindsay Catalla-Buscaino

Rae Fox-Charles draws from diverse expertise to bring culturally-responsive antiracist arts education to students across Greater Minnesota as the Minnesota Department of Education's Arts & Equity Specialist. She earned a BFA in Dance with honors from the Tisch School at NYU, a Master's in Educational Leadership & Policy from University of Michigan, and is a PhD Candidate in the University of Minnesota's Arts in Education program.

Chelsea Gabel is Metis from Rivers, Manitoba, Canada and a Citizen of the Manitoba Metis Federation. Dr. Gabel is an Associate Professor in the Department of Health, Aging and Society and the Indigenous Studies Department at McMaster University. She holds a Canada Research Chair in Indigenous Well-Being, Community-Engagement and Innovation. Her areas of research include Indigenous health and well-being, digital technology, arts-based research, and intergenerational communication.

Marnina Gonick is Professor of Education and Women and Gender Studies at Mount St Vincent University, Halifax, Nova Scotia. She is the author of *Between Femininities: Identity, Ambivalence*, and the *Education of Girls*, published by SUNY Press and the co-author of *Young Femininity: Girlhood, Power and Social Change* published by Palgrave. She is also the co-editor of the book, *Becoming Girl: Collective Biography and the Production of Girlhood*. Her articles have appeared in journals such as Feminist Media Studies, and Gender and Education.

DaVonna Graham

Reyila Hadeer is a PhD candidate in the College of Education at Michigan State University. She studies transnational education from a critical and non-western Indigenous perspective. She is committed to expanding human creativity in (re)creating a more inclusive global community. Reyila believes aesthetic revolution is the foundation of social revolution, and her current research draws on arts-based methods to explore a decolonial notion curriculum from aglobal perspective.

Robert Henry is Métis and citizen of Métis Nation-Saskatchewan, Assistant Professor University of Saskatchewan and holds a Canada Research Chair in Indigenous Justice and Wellbeing

Valerie Kinloch is the Renée and Richard Goldman Dean of the School of Education at the University of Pittsburgh. She is Co-Chair of Remake Learning, Past President of NCTE, and a member of the Board of Trustees of Johnson C. Smith University. She is author of publications on race, literacy, and equity. Her book, *Harlem On Our Minds: Place, Race, and the Literacies of Urban Youth*, received the 2010 AERA Outstanding Book of the Year award. Her new co-authored book is *Where is the Justice? Engaged Pedagogies in Schools and Communities*.

About the Authors

Amanda LaVallee is a Red River Métis from Saskatchewan. She is an Assistant Professor, School of Social Work at the University of Victoria. Her research focus is on the health and well-being of Métis people, specifically on their engagement within social systems and their impact on relationships.

Claudia Mitchell

Richardo Montelongo

Dr. Xuan Thuy Nguyen is an Associate Professor in the Institute of Interdisciplinary Studies and the Feminist Institute for Social Transformation at Carleton University in Canada. Her work has been published in many peer-review journals such as Disability & Society, Disability and the Global South, Global Studies of Childhood, Foucault Studies, and Girlhood Studies: An Interdisciplinary Journal. She is author of *The Journey to Inclusion* (2015, Sense/Brill Publishers).

Asha Omar is an educator, scholar, and artist. She uses art as a tool of resistance, self-expression, and self-love. She enjoys pulling from life experiences to challenge dominant narratives represented in art. Using her background as an artist, she am specifically interested in the ways arts-based methods can portray truths that have traditionally been marginalized and offer a platform for others who may not have the words to convey their experiences.

James Salvo's research interests are in systems of information, communications, data ethics, podcasting as scholarly discourse, and technology as an educational context.

Dr. Leslie C. Sotomayor II, is an artist, curator, and educator. Her dual Ph.Ds in Art Education and Women's, Gender, & Sexuality Studies from The Pennsylvania State University. Sotomayor focuses on Gloria Anzaldúa's theory of conocimiento and autohistoria-teoría, a feminist writing practice of theorizing one's experiences as transformative acts to guide her teaching methodology and curate curriculum for empowerment.

Aaron Teo is a PhD Candidate and Sessional Academic in the University of Queensland's School of Education and a Business/Law teacher at a Brisbane-based Independent School. Aaron's research focusses on the raced and gendered subjectivities of migrant teachers from "Asian" backgrounds in the Australian context, as well as critical pedagogies in white Australian (university and school) classroom spaces. He is interested in qualitative research methods, particularly the use of critical autoethnography as a form of reflexive, emancipatory inquiry.

Thong Vang is a 1.5-generation HMoob American scholar. His family resettled in the U.S. due to the Secret War in Laos. Thong is a Ph.D. candidate in the Culture and Teaching Program at the University of Minnesota - Twin Cities. His research focuses on HMoob ways of being and knowing within HMoob education.

Joanne Yoo is a senior lecturer at the School of Education at the University of Technology Sydney. Her research interests include developing collaborative school partnerships, teaching as an embodied practice, action research and arts-based research methodologies. She is particularly interested in writing as inquiry forms, such as autoethnography. She continues to write creatively within academia to better understand the links between academic inquiry and human flourishing.

Index

A
a posteriori empiricism, 3
academic competency/rigor, 122
activism for self and others, 121
American education foundations, 115–118
antiracist elementary school, 103
arts-based research, 8, 42, 95, 161, 163
   co-creation of knowledge, 46
   community-led solutions, 46
   healing, 72–73, 96–97, 161–163
   theater to empower, 38–39
   see also cellphilming, conocimiento
Ata Bey/Divine Mother, 69–70, 72
ating kuwento, 25, 29
autoethnography, 75, 133
autohistoria-teoria, 7, 59

B
bayanihan/community spirit, 28
BIPOC/Black, Indigenous, People of Color, 35, 101–102, 108, 111
border art/artist(s)/crosser, 63–65, 72–73, 92
Borikên (Puerto Rico's Indigenous name), 73
Borromean knot, 1, 5

C
care and kindness, 78, 119
caste systems, 35, 155–156
cellphilming, 152–153, 156
collaborative spaces, 59,
collective consciousness, 25, 37, 67
conocimiento, 7, 58, 73
construct informed responses, 76
constructivism, 117
Convention on the Rights of Persons with Disabilities, 149
COVID-19 impact, 41, 52, 134
creative acts, 58
critical disability studies, 147
critical reflectiveness, 122-123
cultural empowerment, 25
culturally competent teachers, 115, 121–123, 127–128, 131
culturally relevant pedagogy (CRP)/skills, 8, 102, 107–108, 128

curadora/curandera, 57, 72

D
data analysis, 125
   using interactive model, 125
data collection, 125
   with thick-descriptive paradigms, 125
decentering Whiteness/decolonizing, 16–18, 60, 109, 112–113, 140, 161
decolonial disability studies, 148–151, 160
DEI (diversity, equality, inclusion), 1, 10
   as ethics, v, 1–8
DEIJ (diversity, equity, inclusion, justice), 10–22
Dewey, John, 116, 122
digital storytelling (DST), 41, 46–47
Digital Storytelling Project (DSP), 41
Disabled People's Organizations (DPOs), 151
diversity, 4, 16
   theorizing for institutional change, 11
   ways maintaining status quo, 12
Diversity Requirement Courses (DRC), 12–13, 18
do no harm, 75, 85–86

E
educational inequities/disparities/discrimination, 28, 33, 37
empathy/emotional awareness, 81–83, 127
epistemology, 6–8, 112, 160
Educational Preparation Programs (EPPs), 123, 128–130
English Language Learners (ELLs), 121, 131
equity pedagogy, 120, 137–138
essentialism, 116
ethics, 4, 130
eudaimonism/highest good for all, 3–4, 6, 123

F
Filipino American Student Associations, 30
Filipino communities, 25, 28
   community Elder, 26
First Nations, 41

G
genocide, 35, 62–63
global South, 147–161

H
HMoob, 103, 106–107, 113
history, teaching/bridging contexts, 35, 59
human experiences of change,
human rights/relationships, 135–137

I
Indigenous research, 42
   community-engaged, 42
inclusion, 5, 128
   see also DEI, DEIJ
inquiry-based learning initiatives, 123
Inuit, 41

J
Justice Circles, 103

K
kitchen table talk, 49
knowledge creation, 34
kuwento(s), 29, 35, 38
   see also ating kuwento
Kuwento Co., LLC, 38

L
language for spoken stories, 26
Latina/o/x, 27, 34
Latinx Network (LN) Writers Group, 36
learning never stops, 130, 141
LGBTQIA+, 12
listen intently, 18
lived experience(s), 5, 13, 36, 57, 77, 82, 92, 102, 150

M
male privilege, 138–140
marginalized communities, 12, 140, 151
meaning-making, 85, 118
mentoring, 129–130
metaphor(s), 1, 62–63
methodological frameworks, 7
   advocates for students, 124
   cellphilming, 152, 158
   critical disability studies, 147–153
   digital storytelling, 46
   kitchen table talk, 49

narrative inquiry, 38
Participatory Visual Materials (PVM), 151–158
poetic photographic inquiry, 95–97
spiritual inquiry as symbology, 59, 63
storying, 10, 13–17,
theory of identity, 118–119
visual inquiry/pláticas, 64–72, 95–96
writing as inquiry, 81–85
Métis, 7, 41–45
Mexican American communities, 25
"Mexican schools" in Texas, 31–32, 38
multicultural education, 11, 131

N
Nahuatl, 58
narrative inquiry, 33–34, 38
narrative writing, 76–81
National Center for Education Statistics, 25
   data on doctorates, 25
nepantla/in-between space(s), 58, 67
NVivo qualitative data analysis software, 126

O
OCAP™ (ownership, access, control, possession), 41, 54
online research platforms, 42, 48
   adaptations, 53
open to new ways of inquiry, 86
oral histories/storytelling traditions, 14, 27, 33–34, 47, 153–156

P
perennialism, 115
philosophical underpinnings, 115
poetic photographic inquiry, 89, 95
Port Royal Experiment, 117–118
praxis, 133
prescriptive curriculum/mandated testing, 124
problem-solving initiatives, 123
professional identity development, 120, 130
progressivism, 116–117
PVM (Participatory Visual Materials), 151–161
   see also methodological frameworks
PWIs/predominantly White institutions, 12, 17, 21

Q
qualitative research, 25–27, 34, 81, 121–130

R
racial dominance in education spaces, 31–33
racial healing, 104–105
  see also arts-based research
racism, 31–32, 37, 133
reflexive conceptual framework, 76
  journaling, 37
  to drive learning, 80, 128
research ethics, 7, 41
relational accountability, 49–52
restorying/reflecting on storying, 20–22, 9, 156–159
  see also oral histories
romanticism/naturalism, 116

S
scholar activist, 102
scholar practitioner, 36
self-knowledge/efficacy, 59–61, 119, 126–128
sexism, 135–142
Spanglish, 37
spiral significance, 64
spirit of inquiry, 91, 122
standing apart, 83–85
storying/storytelling, 9, 25, 39, 52, 104
  see also autoethnography, autohistoria-teoria, conocimiento, kuwento, oral history, testimonio
supportive feedback, 75, 80

T
Tagalog, 26
Taglish, 37
Taíno, 57, 62–53, 69, 73
testimonio(s), 7, 25, 27, 35, 38, 57, 60
transformative recursive process, 58–60
Transforming Disability Knowledge, Research and Activism (TDKRA), 150–158
transnational education, 92
Tri-Council Policy Statement 2 (TCPS 2), 41, 53–54

U
universal accessibility/rights, 1, 5–6
Utuado, Puerto Rico, 57, 65, 70
Uyghurs, 89–90, 97–98

V
Vietnam, 149–151, 153–158

visual inquiry, 93–95
visual pláticas, 57, 67